THE DIGITAL TRANSFORMATION PLAYBOOK

WHAT YOU NEED TO KNOW AND DO

D1484299

Library of Congress Control Number:
2023933855

ISBN:
978-1-62825-781-6 (Paperback)
978-1-62825-782-3 (eBook)

Published by:
Project Management Institute, Inc.
18 Campus Blvd., Ste. 150
Newtown Square, Pennsylvania 19073-3299 USA
Phone: +1 610 356 4600
Email: customercare@pmi.org
Internet: PMI.org

THE DIGITAL TRANSFORMATION PLAYBOOK

WHAT YOU NEED TO KNOW AND DO

PMI.org
brightline.org
thinkers50.com

Project Management Institute.

Brightline Project Management Institute.

THINKERS 50

Contents

1   **Innovation at Speed and Scale: Competing in the Digital Era with the Flywheel Operating Model**
Charles Gildehaus, David Allred, Allison Bailey, Amanda Luther, and Sesh Iyer

13   **Walk Before You Run: A Learning Curve in Digital Transformation**
Didier Bonnet

19   **Are You Willing and Ready to Embrace AI?**
Antonio Nieto-Rodriguez and Ricardo Viana Vargas

25   **The Heart of Digital Transformation**
Scott D. Anthony and Paul Cobban

35   **The Digital Transformation Imperative**
Emil Andersson, Tahirou Assane Oumarou, and Tony O'Driscoll

45   **Pipelines to Platforms to Protocols: Reconfiguring Value and Redesigning Markets**
Sangeet Paul Choudary

53   **Securing Innovation and Antifragility as Part of Your Digital Transformation Strategy**
Vincenzo Corvello and Annika Steiber

59   **How Established Companies Can Surf New Tech Waves**
Elisa Farri and Fabio Veronese

67   **Joint Action Model**
Janka Krings-Klebe and Jörg Schreiner

75   **Overcoming the Resistance to Behavioral Change**
Kaihan Krippendorff

85   **Preempting Digital Disruption: The Nightmare Competitor Contest**
Kurt Matzler, Christian Stadler, and Julia Hautz

95   **Beyond Digital: Why Reimagination Is the New Execution**
Terence Mauri

103　**Citizen Development: Bridging the Gap Between the Business and IT**
　　　Dalibor Ninkovic and Laura Faughtenberry

113　**The Five Questions to Answer in Your Digitalization Strategy**
　　　Josef Oehmen and Udo Hielscher

123　**The Why of Digital Transformation**
　　　Martin Reeves and Adam Job

131　**How to Design and Unlock the Strategic Value of Your Transformation Office**
　　　Andrew Schuster, Karsten Kuhrmeier, Julie McClean, and Samuel Pownall

141　**Transformation in a Digital World**
　　　Robin Speculand

147　**The Digital Transformation of Industrial Firms: What, Why, and How**
　　　Annika Steiber

155　**Rethinking Business for the Digital Age**
　　　Shekhar Tankhiwale and Habeeb Mahboob

165　**AI-Powered ESG: Our Chance to Make a Real Difference?**
　　　Terence Tse, Mark Esposito, and Danny Goh

175　**Disrupting the Disruptors: How Human Capital Makes or Breaks Digital Innovation**
　　　Ricardo Viana Vargas

Foreword

Digital transformation has become an imperative. In today's fast-paced, digital-first world, businesses of all sizes and industries must embrace digital technologies in order to stay competitive and relevant. This is true for a small business in Oregon just as much as it is for a large corporation in South Korea.

Successful digital transformation is a journey that requires a deep understanding of both technology and people. It is not just about investing in the latest tech tools but about finding the right technology for your business and then using it to transform your processes, people, and culture. The *Digital Transformation Playbook: What You Need to Know and Do*, created by the Brightline® Initiative of Project Management Institute and Thinkers50, offers a selection of insights and experiences from world-leading thinkers, as well as practical tools and frameworks to help leaders to deal with this complex and demanding process.

While digital transformation can lead to growth, scale, efficiency, and expansion for businesses of all sizes, it requires a commitment to learning and experimentation and the ability to adapt and pivot as needed. You will also need to consider the impact that digital technologies will have on your organization. Ultimately, digital transformation is about driving business growth and success by use of technology. It is about finding new and innovative ways to deliver value to your customers and to stay ahead of the competition. With the right tools, strategies, and mindset, you can emerge stronger and more competitive than ever before.

I believe *The Digital Transformation Playbook: What You Need to Know and Do* will be a valuable resource for you and your organization as you embark on this exciting and challenging journey.

Pierre Le Manh
President and CEO, Project Management Institute

Innovation at Speed and Scale: Competing in the Digital Era with the Flywheel Operating Model

CHARLES GILDEHAUS, DAVID ALLRED, ALLISON BAILEY, AMANDA LUTHER, AND SESH IYER

1

Digital technologies are driving a rapid and irreversible shift in the basis of business competition—continuous customer-centric innovation, at speed and scale, is now the name of the game. Market-leading incumbents are now confronting the limitations of their conventional top-down, control-centric operating model. Digital leaders, on the other hand, have embraced this sea change; and are pioneering a new operating model—the flywheel—powered by innovative product teams and an accompanying shift in culture and governance to support them.

Digital Is Shifting the Basis of Business Competition

Digital is shifting the basis of business competition. Customer and employee expectations continue to rise. Competitive pressure from new entrants and new forms of competition are intensifying. Globalization continues to amplify the volatility, complexity, and uncertainty of the interconnected global economy. To compete and win in this new environment companies must learn, adapt, and innovate faster than their competition. Innovation at speed, and at scale, is the new name of the game.

Digital leaders have embraced this new reality. They are systematically harnessing digital technologies to drive innovation velocity in every part of their business. They are deploying artificial intelligence (AI) and digital solutions to create user-centric learning loops to gather data, generate insights, and continuously reshape and reinvent customer experiences, as well as core operations. They understand, at a very intuitive level, the power of digital to augment and accelerate the basic loop of human learning.

Digital leaders have pioneered a new product-centric, digital-first operating model, built around this foundational premise, which we call the flywheel. This operating model prioritizes product teams and empowers them to drive continuous value delivery along every element of the business's value chain. These multidisciplinary teams leverage AI- and digital-powered solutions to create powerful self-reinforcing loops for continuous data-driven innovation. Once spinning, these virtuous cycles act like flywheels, creating their own momentum for always-on reinvention and growth. This flywheel effect also creates transformative energy for the entire organization, enabling the test-and-learn mindset and ways of working to permeate the culture and take root across the organization.

A Boston Consulting Group (BCG) study of 1,200 global companies vividly illustrates the power of this model. From 2018 to 2021, the companies that pioneered and scaled this digital-first operating model delivered 2.5 times higher total shareholder value overall (Forth et al., 2022).

Limitations of the Conventional Operating Model

Since the early days of the industrial age, operating models have been continuously refined and optimized to enable business leaders to drive scale while maintaining tight operational control and minimizing risk. Functional hierarchies, top-down planning, restricted decision-making abilities, and multilayered approval mechanisms are all logical components of this model. This system was ideal for competing in the scale-oriented marketplaces of the 20th century, when operating at lower cost across broader markets was the primary determinant of market share and profitability.

The inherent limitation of this model is that it actively restricts broad-based experimentation and test-and-learn innovation. In fact, as these systems are built out over time, becoming ever more sprawling and intricate, they trigger a set of dynamics that severely handicap a company's ability to keep pace and compete in the digital era.

The first dynamic is a disconnection from the customer. As functional hierarchies grow larger, they tend to become more rigid, pushing decision-making authority up the hierarchy and away from where customer interactions take place. In this system, no single team or leader owns the full end-to-end product and customer experience, making it exceedingly difficult to implement customer-centric innovations quickly and effectively. As a result, frontline employees, who have the insights and inspiration to drive innovations where they are needed most, grow disillusioned and disempowered over time. Each time a team member comes up with a new idea, they are forced to push through a brutal gauntlet of approvals to get anything done. As this pattern repeats itself, teams and individuals eventually lose their will to innovate; the pain isn't worth the gain.

The second dynamic is diminished velocity—the speed at which decisions are made and then translated into action and business outcomes. Scaling a business drives exponential growth in its organizational and technical dependencies. In an attempt to control and manage this complexity, organizations add layer upon layer of mechanisms for prioritization, approval, and coordination. As senior managers sink more and more of their energy into navigating this path—seeking alignment and sitting on committees—they inevitably hit a tipping point, spending more time on these activities than on driving value for the business.

The third dynamic is the set of encumbrances and barriers that develop around the technology organization, isolating it as a standalone functional empire. Business leaders now recognize that bridging this historical divide— completely rethinking and reinventing the way technology teams integrate and interface with the core business—is an absolute strategic imperative. This requires driving a transformational shift in how technology is deployed, from an IT-driven approach to a business-driven one. It entails moving beyond a multiyear big bang IT-project orientation to a continuous-value-delivery orientation centered on products. Senior leaders in the technology organization—those most often tasked with tackling this transformation—face a complex tripartite challenge:

1. Modernizing their technology infrastructure to drive new efficiencies and create new levels of flexibility and modularity; while

2. Building new human capabilities within their organization, such as new digital ways of working, improved culture, and updated skills; and

3. Meeting the business leaders where they are and facilitating changes on their side.

Successfully meeting these challenges is no small feat.

Countless companies have turned to the agile movement as a panacea for these problems. There is no doubt that the vast majority of these implementations have laid a critical foundation for executing iterative, sprint-based software development. Agile has successfully delivered substantial gains in engineering velocity, yet many of these transformations fail to address the underlying structures at the root of the traditional command-and-control operating model. Many of these efforts have thus fallen short of the original aspiration to build a new set of capabilities to deliver continuous customer-centric innovation. In short, agile initiatives have proven highly effective in teaching teams *how to* build but not nearly as effective in teaching teams *what to* build.

The Flywheel Operating Model

The flywheel is an evolution of the conventional operating model—embraced by those who recognize that today's companies can't win with yesterday's assumptions. The flywheel enables organizations to systematically harness digital technologies to drive rapid, iterative, and continuous learning and innovation across the business value chain, with equal priority on cost efficiencies and new revenue growth. This evolution retains the cost, efficiency, and control elements of the conventional model but pushes them down to a foundational level. The flywheel has four interconnected components that empower frontline teams to drive innovation at speed and at scale as described in the following subsections.

Product Primacy

Digital leaders deploy teams to capture high-value opportunities and invent new end-to-end solutions or products. (See the sidebar, "Defining *Product*.") These teams are empowered to drive iterative, user-centric innovation of those solutions in order to continuously deliver value to the business. Digital leaders recognize that each of these products is a nexus, or interaction point, between the business and the customer or end user where value is continually created. For this reason, they elevate *product* as the primary axis, around which all resources, processes, capabilities, assets, and technologies are organized.

The resulting management philosophy is called *product primacy*. Product teams at the center of this model are multidisciplinary— armed with product, design, data science, engineering skills and talent—and have full responsibility for the end-to-end life cycle of the product and the value stream associated with that product. The product manager leading the team is responsible for driving the dynamic evolution of a product roadmap and for enabling their team to deliver specific outcomes that culminate in the key results the business has committed to its investors.

These teams are bolstered by the tight integration of other critical functions that are needed to support the product such as marketing, legal and compliance, and manufacturing. In addition, the organization's planning, governance, and funding processes are reoriented to embrace product-platform orientation and provide decision-making autonomy to the business, product, and technology leaders responsible for these teams.

Defining *Product*

Digital leaders embrace a broad and encompassing definition of product. A product is a tool, a solution, or an experience that solves a problem for the end user and thereby creates utility and value. This definition includes the primary good or service the company sells to its customers but it stretches beyond this to embrace digital experiences (e.g., digital on-boarding journey for a new customer), digital platforms (e.g., a video service platform), and internal digital solutions (e.g., a workforce management application). What all of these have in common is that they are the interaction point between the business and the customer/end user, and thus the nexus of value creation. Digital leaders also embrace the fact that all physical products will eventually incorporate or integrate a digital element (e.g., digital twins being used to drive product innovation for an automotive parts manufacturer or a sensor-driven AI-model to predict failure in a transformer on an energy grid).

Data-Driven, Continuous, Customer-Centric Innovation

If job number one for a product team is to invent a breakthrough product, then job number two is to drive ongoing user-centric innovation around that new product to ensure it continuously delivers value. Digital leaders have created a playbook for doing this. In a recent study of digital native companies, we interviewed more than 50 product officers and digital product managers at leading digital native companies, identifying the common operating blueprint these leaders deploy to drive successive rounds of data-driven innovation on their teams. This playbook integrates the foundational approaches of design thinking, lean, and agile into a process aimed at driving a virtuous cycle of end-user engagement, learning, and innovation. It has four steps:

Build knowledge of the end user through feedback. Integrate quantitative and qualitative data so that the flywheel team can easily access it in real time. Leadership must set clear guardrails and protocols for personal data and privacy as these are essential elements for guiding actions and decision-making.

Generate insights using an analytical toolkit and set of routines. Uncover new value by identifying where the biggest opportunities lie.

Run experiments. Generate innovative solutions by structuring rigorous, rapid tests that monitor impact, drive key performance indicators (KPIs), and eliminate waste and dead ends.

Build and deploy. Build and deploy agile software development routines and full production support processes to enable rapid and continuous delivery of enhancements to products, services, and platforms.

Digital leaders have developed and refined a set of subprocesses and tools that enable their product teams to execute each of these steps as part of a rigorous and efficient routine, operating on a weekly, monthly, and quarterly cadence. The playbook is specifically designed to empower each of the product team's disciplines—business, product, design, engineering, data science—to lead, drive, and contribute to each of the four steps. In these ways, the playbook represents a revolutionary way of working—integrating the principles of multidisciplinary teamwork and data-driven discipline into a single cohesive model.

Platform Technology Orientation

Digital technology is the foundational enabler of this four-step playbook. Interacting with end users through the digital medium means massively accelerating the speed at which product teams communicate, run test-and-learn experiments, capture data, and build knowledge about the end user. AI means massively accelerating the speed at which product teams learn, generate new insights, and apply them to create value for the end user. For this reason, to be successful, product teams need a fluid, modular, and flexible technology environment in which to operate, where access to data, microservices, and expertise enables them to move quickly and creatively to drive continuous test-and-learn innovation.

The challenge for many market-leading incumbents is how to transform their technology organization to deliver this environment—how to overcome the inherent limitations and encumbrances, described earlier, around legacy infrastructure, ways of working, governance, culture, and talent. Digital leaders who have successfully made this transition have deployed a three-part formula:

Business-platform teams. Reorganize enterprise technologies into business platforms, which represent a collection of applications working in concert to achieve key outcomes. Business platforms are typically aligned with a company's core operations and may include many complementary applications and cloud services. Creating such a tight linkage between the way a company operates and its supporting technologies dramatically improves visibility into technology potential and return on investment. Technology delivery must be executed by dedicated end-to-end business and technology teams responsible for defining requirements and executing development. Success is defined not by delivering on time and on budget, but by raising team expectations to achieving the targeted business KPIs.

Technology-platform teams. Create teams that are responsible for empowering product teams to become more autonomous (and requiring far greater IT support) by leveraging configurable technology and data services. Technology-platform teams are focused on anticipating and creating the tools and application programming interfaces (APIs) that will be in high demand from product teams, and modernizing the necessary underlying systems and tools without compromising security, cost, or scalability. Success of the technology-platform team is determined by its ability to ensure that business-platform teams have greater innovation latitude and can operate with greater speed and agility. They do this by delivering a powerful library of reusable APIs and microservices that can be used in digital product development; highly usable data that is systematic, centralized, integrated, cleaned, and broadly available; and a centralized and standardized infrastructure that is secure and can maximize the overall return on technology investment.

With these resources at their disposal, product teams are free to focus on high-value objectives such as creating exceptional customer experiences or leveraging AI to automate business processes. Ideally, this feels more like compiling preexisting technology services made available by the platform teams than having each team creating its own base technologies.

Modular data and digital platform architecture. Build a tiered, modular data and digital platform (DDP) architecture designed to liberate data from inflexible legacy systems and empower business users to create new use case solutions. The DDP architecture decouples technology into the layers outlined below as a way to separate responsibilities and minimize complex dependencies:

- **Multichannel front-end and product modules.** Enable reusability of components and shared features to optimize app development across a variety of user interfaces.
- **Integration and interoperability.** Ensure the integration of third parties, products, and core systems via APIs and standardized middleware.
- **Infrastructure.** Provide an optimized hybrid infrastructure that combines the best of cloud and on-premise capabilities.
- **Data and analytics.** Build a modern, centralized data-storage solution and enable data sharing across systems and products.
- **Security.** Protect sensitive data and information and ensure high standards for privacy and compliance.

Empowerment Leadership and Governance Model

The final component of the flywheel model is empowering product teams by pushing decision-making authority downward and outward to encourage experimentation, learning, and continuous innovation.

Single-threaded leadership (STL) is an organizational approach designed to maximize ownership, empowerment, and accountability by providing more autonomy to teams. Amazon pioneered and scaled the STL model in the 2010s, when its leadership recognized that exponential growth had put the company on the path of death-spiral bureaucracy. Senior managers were seeing yellow flags: leaders whose attention was fragmented, stalled initiatives, and frustrated and disempowered teams. Most alarming was the realization that Amazon's innovation velocity—the competitive weapon it had used so effectively to disrupt and upend the retail giants—was beginning to dwindle (Bryar et al., 2021).

The retail giant set out on a multiyear journey to completely reinvent its management system, starting with the idea that business leaders would be assigned a single initiative or business problem. Leaders were given end-to-end ownership to deliver on their primary objectives and would spend all of their time, energy, and talent finding a way to make it happen. Amazon called these individuals "single-threaded leaders" (a reference to a single-threaded program, which executes one stream of commands at a time). Amazon then instituted single-threaded teams (STTs). Senior management empowered these autonomous, multidisciplinary teams to decide the best way to fulfill their mission and gave them the skills, roles, and resources to deliver on it.

The flywheel teams described here are the natural evolution of STTs.

The most critical element of this new structure is designing teams that are truly separable: eliminating, or at least massively reducing, the organizational and technical dependencies required to execute their plans, so they no longer needed to align, coordinate, wait on, or block other teams. In this way, the single-threaded model targets the root structural issue—a complex web of interdependencies—which underlies most of the challenges facing traditional governance models.

Amazon's implementation is the purest and most complete manifestation of an empowerment-oriented leadership and governance model. While it isn't appropriate for every company, its guiding principles—increased autonomy, reduced dependencies, refocused leaders, and empowered teams—serve as useful guideposts for an incumbent organization looking to evolve. How best to apply these elements will depend on unique contextual circumstances, including leadership, culture, talent, and the technological orientation of the business.

Getting Started

Over the past decade, thousands of companies have launched full-scale, end-to-end digital transformation initiatives that have proven notoriously difficult to navigate. A BCG study of more than 800 companies found that nearly 76% of digital transformation initiatives fail to achieve their stated objectives (Forth et al., 2020).

The pitfalls are well-known—long time lines, fatigue, failure to demonstrate a return, resistance from middle management, employee skepticism, senior leadership transitions, and, perhaps most common, collapse under the overwhelming complexity and scope of the transformation. Yet they all remain stubbornly difficult to avoid. Even the label *transformation* can be problematic. When it comes to digital, there is no real beginning, no real end, and certainly no straight lines.

The flywheel offers an alternative, evolutionary approach to navigating the change effort—one that is iterative and ongoing, where learning is the currency, and adaptation the norm. To get started, companies should consider three practical guidelines:

Start small (but think big). Transformation efforts typically kick off big, bold programs with fanfare and a heavy investment. Start instead by picking one tangible problem—a point of customer friction or operational inefficiency, perhaps—with obvious potential to unlock value, then task a single team to solve it in a novel way. Assemble a multidisciplinary flywheel team, empower its members to follow playbook principles, and challenge them to invent a new solution. Clear the runway for the team to build and launch their product and create business impact as fast as possible.

Demonstrate value to leadership. Flywheel teams must build something useful quickly and get it into the hands of users so the team can get feedback, adjust, and make iterative improvements. Leadership must therefore provide flywheel teams with the license to start testing their concepts with customers immediately. This creates two sources of momentum: it requires the team to demonstrate business impact and primes executive leadership to view and reinforce the success of the flywheel model.

Build on successes to scale the flywheel across the organization. The original product team can serve as proof of the flywheel concept. Once this value is realized, management should empower other flywheel teams to build products based on the original team's approach. Build out management systems and reporting mechanisms to encourage flywheel activity across all products and clear away command-and-control obstacles. Encourage and fund the technology-platform team to create the portfolio of bulletproof services that the flywheel teams will need for their technology development. In this way, the first team serves as a Minimum Viable Operating Model—to accelerate the organization learning about what works and better understand the barriers and blockers that will need to be overcome to enable the organization to fully scale the flywheel operating model at the enterprise level.

Operating Model Implications

The flywheel operating model offers companies a new perspective and fresh approach to how they operate, transform, and win in the market. The four core elements describe what digital leaders do exceptionally well and what it takes to drive innovation at speed and at scale across an organization. Because of this, the flywheel serves as a North Star, providing businesses with a consistent direction and a coherent framework for execution.

The transformative potential of the flywheel approach extends across every critical element of the enterprise, spanning culture and talent, organizational design, ways of working, and technology. A full discussion on the implications of the flywheel could fill a good-sized book, but by customizing this approach to the specific needs of a company, an executive can begin to tap into the momentum offered by the flywheel operating model.

This article is the second in the Innovation Flywheel Series. The first article, *Powering the Innovation Flywheel in the Digital Era*, introduces the concept of the innovation flywheel and presents the four-step playbook used by digital-native product teams to drive continuous customer-centric innovation. This article presents an operating model, pioneered by digital leaders across every industry, as a North Star to guide the digital transformation journey for market-leading incumbents seeking to build the capabilities they need to compete and win in the digital era.

References

Bryar, C., & Carr, B., (2021). *Working backwards: Insights, stories, and secrets from inside Amazon.* St Martin's Press.

Forth, P., de Laubier, R., Chakraborty, S., Charanya, T., & Magagnoli, M. (2022). *The rise of the digital incumbent.* BCG. https://www.bcg.com/publications/2022/rise-of-digital-incumbents-building-digital-capabilities

Forth, P., Reichert, T., de Laubier, R., & Chakraborty, S. (2020). *Flipping the odds of digital transformation success.* BCG. https://www.bcg.com/publications/2020/increasing-odds-of-success-in-digital-transformation

About the Authors

Charles Gildehaus is a Managing Director and Partner at BCG. He co-founded BCG Digital Ventures (BCG DV), Boston Consulting Group's corporate venture investment and incubation firm. He focuses on advising CEOs and senior executives across the industry on digital innovation, transformation, and new business build.

David Allred is a Managing Director and Senior Partner at BCG. He co-founded BCG Digital Ventures (BCG DV), Boston Consulting Group's corporate venture investment and incubation firm. David has launched over 20 successful ventures with corporate partners across TMT, automotive and mobility, building materials, insurance, energy, and medtech.

Allison Bailey is a Managing Director and Senior Partner at BCG. She is the Global Leader of the firm's People and Organization Practice Area and is an experienced transformation leader, helping companies implement large-scale change, including organization redesign, digital transformation, operational improvement, and post-merger integration.

Amanda Luther is a Managing Director and Partner at BCG. She co-leads Digital Transformation globally and is a member of the Technology and Digital Advantage leadership team. Amanda is an expert on digital, data, and advanced analytics topics, serving clients in industries including retail, restaurants, Consumer Packaged Goods, travel and tourism, and the public sector.

Sesh Iyer is a Managing Director and Senior Partner at BCG and the North American regional cochair for BCG X, Boston Consulting Group's tech build and design unit. He also leads the firm's work in the Americas in lean services and operations in technology and IT, and cloud computing.

Walk Before You Run: A Learning Curve in Digital Transformation

DIDIER BONNET

f various studies from academics, consultants, and analysts are to be believed, the rate of digital transformations failing to meet their original objectives ranges from 70% to 95%, with an average at 87.5% (Wade & Shan, 2020). That is surely enough to scare away most rational investors or risk-conscious business leaders! Yet digital transformation has been at the top of corporate agendas for at least a decade and shows no sign of slowing down. On the contrary, many commentators have highlighted the accelerating impact of the COVID-19 pandemic on digital transformation adoption. So, why are such bad odds not deterring the corporate fixation with digital transformation? Our research points to three main reasons for this poor outlook. The first two are straightforward and involve objective setting and falling into traditional pitfalls in transformation. The third reason is less obvious. There is a learning curve in digital transformation and many firms are ignoring it.

The problem with firms failing to meet their digital transformation objectives is often about early objectives setting (if done at all) and over-optimistic expectations of both the timing and scope of the outcome. The over-promise of digital transformation as the magic wand to solving most organizational and business problems, leads to senior leaders' over-optimistic expectations of what their organizations could deliver. You'd think that after a decade of digital transformation, lessons would have been learned! Not quite. The dominant narrative about digital transformation is still framed around the transformational potential of digital technology. Whereas the possibilities brought about by technologies, such as artificial intelligence (AI) and machine learning (ML), are not in question, the hype around the timing of their impact on transforming traditional businesses certainly is. Technology-led digital change is not a short-cycle transformation.

The second aspect behind digital transformation failures is more troubling. Over the last decade, we've made some good progress in understanding the people and organizational components that drive successful digital transformation (Westerman et al., 2014). Yet, many organizations are still falling into the same old traps. Lack of proper governance, technology deployment over user adoption, wrong metrics, and the like, still hinder execution. Research from the International Institute for Management Development (IMD, 2021) shows that 61% of companies still have a fragmented approach to their digital transformations, up from 53% in 2019. So it is no surprise the benefits from digital investments are not producing the results as hoped.

The third hurdle has to do with the pace of leading and managing the transition between the old and the new. Digital leaders must be ambidextrous, exploiting and optimizing the existing operations while exploring new sources of digital growth to secure the future prosperity of their organizations. But at what pace and with what balance of investment? Of course, the nature of competition and the level of industry disruption can often dictate the pace. In many cases we've studied, however, there was a strong disconnect between the strategic focus of companies' digital ambitions and the actual digital maturity needed for their organizations to deliver. During a recent interview, the CEO of a large consumer goods organization described her digital strategy as entirely based on data-driven decision-making and centered on building a digital platform, where customers could buy the company's products as well as a number of complementary products from ecosystem partners. Discussions with the chief data officer (CDO) and the chief information officer (CIO) painted a slightly different picture. Both described a complex and difficult program of integrating disparate customer databases and establishing a middleware to structure data in a way that could be used for commercial decision-making and both projected two to three years for completion. Isn't this running before you can walk?

Of course, transformational digital ambitions are a good thing and need to be encouraged but only if they are backed by the required investments and ability to raise the digital capability of the organization to execute. Otherwise, this is just wishful thinking. Our conclusion from our research is that there is indeed an organizational learning curve in digital transformation. It's no surprise that companies, often recognized as digital transformation leaders, such as Nike in B2C or Schneider Electric in industrial products, have delivered several transformation cycles and have been doing this for many years.

Awareness of this digital learning curve has become an imperative for senior leaders to succeed in digital transformation. We found three distinct stages in the digital transformation learning curve. The first two, modernization and enterprise-wide transformation, are focused on reshaping the existing business. The last phase is about new business creation and uncovering new sources of value. All three phases present different opportunities for organizational learning, and experience shows that it's hard to avoid significant challenges at each stage.

Modernization is about digitizing existing processes and functions. For customer experience, it can be about designing customer apps or implementing new self-service touchpoints. For operations excellence, it can be about connecting products and digitally reengineering core processes. For employee experience, it can be about automating HR processes or providing a self-service portal for employees. Do these digital programs transform the organization? Most likely not. This phase is often undervalued or even derided but shouldn't be. Just like the foundations of a house, it makes the organization digitally stronger and smarter. It also provides reasonably short returns that can fuel more complex digital investments and it is a great source of organizational learning for connectivity, process automation, and user adoption challenges.

Enterprise-wide transformation is a complex cross-value chain change effort. For customer experience, it can be an omni-channel integration or moving from product-based to customer-centric delivery models. For operations excellence, it can be an Internet of Things (IoT) application for predictive maintenance or automating order to cash processes. For employee experience, it can be institutionalizing agile approaches of working or establishing a continuous learning and reskilling culture. Are these transformational? Absolutely. These have all the hallmarks of true business transformations. Aligning traditional organizational silos, establishing proper governance models, adding new talents and the like, are all critical muscles to develop for transformation success. Enterprise-wide transformations are usually focused on improving existing operations; when successful, they very often open up new value creation opportunities such as extending the reach of the customers we are able to serve or finding new efficient ways of running operations. Enterprise-wide transformations are complex but are mandatory learning phases on the journey to digital transformation maturity.

New business creation is about increasing the size of the existing market or creating new revenue pools that we did not previously address. For customer experience, it can be moving from selling products and services to subscription-based models. For operation excellence, it can be using data and analytics to accurately predict the operational performance of our products or systems. For employee experience, it can be new adaptive models of delivery through talent ecosystems. These are true transformations because they challenge the existing processes, structures, and capabilities of the existing organization and require new ways of working. Leadership is key as this is about transitioning from the existing models of operations to new ones. Often, this phase also demands a rethink of how we define the boundaries of our organizations as we move from traditional linear supply chains to orchestrated ecosystems. The organizational learnings are therefore massive and require a high level of digital transformation maturity.

Are these three digital transformation horizons completely linear? Probably not in the sense that most organizations will manage a portfolio of initiatives that may cover all three areas—for instance, undertaking a certain amount of modernization to deliver quick wins, while at the same time having enterprise-wide global programs and/or innovating business models through experiments and controlled pilots. But from an organizational learning perspective, it's rare not to say impossible, to find examples of digital leaders in large corporations that have leapfrogged over the early phases. Growing your organization's digital maturity through the digital transformation corporate learning curve will increase your chances of success.

My research suggests these are the important learnings for digital leaders:

- Don't underplay *modernization*. Modernization will not transform your organization but it will provide quick wins and allow your customers and employees to start connecting with your organization in different ways. It's a good foundation to build from.
- *Enterprise-wide transformations* are the learning ground for true digital business transformation. They are complex and difficult to execute but a mandatory step in making your organization digitally mature.
- *New business creation* is about building the future of your organization. Unless you decide to pursue a separate venture away from the corporate mothership, it will require a high level of digital maturity to effect and scale the transition successfully.
- *Build a portfolio of initiatives* across all three horizons, but make sure you gain the organizational learning at each stage to increase your digital maturity and maximize your chances of success.

References

International Institute for Management Development (IMD). (2021). *The digital vortex 2021: Digital disruption in a covid world*. IMD Global Center for Digital Business Transformation.

Wade, M., & Shan, J. (2020). *Covid-19 has accelerated digital transformation, but may have made it harder not easier*. MIS Quarterly Executive, 19(3), 213–222.

Westerman, G., Bonnet, D., & McAfee, A. (2014). *Leading digital: Turning technology into business transformation*. Harvard Business Review Press.

About the Author

Dr. Didier Bonnet is Professor of Strategy and Digital Transformation at the International Institute for Management Development (IMD) in Switzerland. He is coauthor of *Leading Digital: Turning Technology into Business Transformation* (Harvard Business Review Press, 2014) and *Hacking Digital: Best Practices to Implement and Accelerate your Business Transformation* (McGraw Hill, 2022).

Are You Willing and Ready to Embrace AI?

ANTONIO NIETO-RODRIGUEZ AND
RICARDO VIANA VARGAS

When it comes to artificial intelligence (AI), project leaders should ask themselves two key questions. First: Are my organization and I willing to adopt AI-inspired tools as part of the ordinary course of doing business, particularly in project management? This question will give you a sense of your organization's appetite for adopting machine learning (ML)–inspired technology. The second—and, in fact, the more critical question—is: Are my organization and I ready to take this important leap forward? This question will give you a sense of how quickly you can identify and apply AI to projects.

The not-so-happy news is that there are many more organizations willing to apply AI to their projects than organizations ready to do it.

Why do so many organizations lag when it comes to being ready? The first limiting factor is a fundamental misunderstanding of the nature of AI and what it can and cannot do for a business. If you are unsure about what AI can do for your business, you are also likely unaware of what you need to do to lay the foundation for AI adoption.

The other limiting factor is a fundamental miscalculation about how people and culture restrict the organization's willingness to adopt AI solutions. Even the best and most up-to-date technologies can be defeated by leaders and workforces gripped by the uninformed fears about the impact technology can have on their lives.

The only thing we can all agree on is that willing and ready or not: AI is coming!

AI Significantly Improves Project Outcomes

It is no exaggeration to suggest that project management is at the heart of business operations and transformations. Just about everything you do in pursuit of success involves a project of one sort or another. The truly successful organizations tend to be those that can devise, design, implement, and complete projects with more certainty.

In case you were wondering, not all organizations have a grasp on those competencies. The Standish Group, which for several decades has charted the success of technology projects, estimates that only one-third of all projects around the world are successful in achieving their goals. Less than one-half of those projects produce high-value returns.

There are a variety of reasons for this, but one thing is clear: the introduction of AI has the potential to massively improve this woeful record of success. If—and it's a big if— organizations are both willing and ready to embrace AI and allow it to come to fruition.

Gartner research suggests that by 2030, 80% of basic project management tasks will be run by AI and powered by big data, ML, and natural language processing.

Additionally, new AI innovations are arriving on what seems like an almost daily basis. For example, the business world has only just familiarized itself with the possible benefits of ChatGPT, an AI-inspired chatbot that powers things such as the new Bing search engine. The first version of ChatGPT was released in November 2022 and by March 2023, its creators had already released GPT-4, a fourth-generation version capable of accepting text and image inputs. The incredibly fast pace of change in AI applications puts a lot of pressure on businesses to keep up.

However, not all organizations have the capacity to use AI to improve their business operations and project management. This lack of readiness can be defined in a number of ways, but at the heart of this failure is the inability to find and harness the power of data.

Data is the Heartbeat of AI Readiness

All AI adoption processes begin with data—lots and lots of data, properly consolidated and organized. AI is only as good as the data you have at your disposal, and if that data does not exist, or is poorly stored and haphazardly organized, then you're going to have trouble migrating from the community of the willing to the community of the ready.

In our research, we found that roughly 80% of the time preparing an ML algorithm is devoted to data gathering and cleaning. That is where we take raw and unstructured data and transform it into structured data that can be used to train an ML model. Once that has been done, the possibilities are nearly endless.

Our own research has shown that, once employed, AI can help organizations select and prioritize the projects they should undertake, identifying launch-ready projects sooner and removing human biases in decision-making.

AI can also help provide faster project scoping, planning, and reporting. It can also help create and implement sophisticated advanced testing systems and software that were once only available to the richest companies engaged in the largest and most costly projects.

Again, however, these dividends are only available if an organization is truly ready to accept and deploy the technology. Currently, we can easily see that there is a broad spectrum of readiness among business organizations—from "all-systems go" to "don't know where to start" orientations.

The AI Readiness Spectrum: A Checklist for Leaders

How can you tell how ready your organization is? The following questions do not touch on all the concerns, but they do capture major issues that must be resolved before you will be truly ready to embrace AI. Be frank in answering each question and give your organization a score, ranging from one (least ready) to five (most ready). If your organization's score falls below 24 (an average score of three on each question), then you have some work to do to build readiness:

1. **Do you have the people and patience to build an accurate inventory of all current and past projects, including the latest status updates?** This is essential information that will help you determine the scope of an AI implementation project.

2. **Do you have the resources to gather, clean, and structure your organization's data?** Many organizations have data on all aspects of business operations, yet it is hidden away in physical file cabinets on paper spreadsheets or stored digitally in different IT platforms. You need all the data collated and organized on a single platform so that you can get a complete picture of your organization's potential for project management success.

3. **How ready is your organization and its people to abandon old management habits, such as monthly progress reports, that will be rendered redundant by AI?** AI possesses great transformational potential, but only if the technology is used the way it was intended to be used. Asking ML models to pump out monthly progress reports in the same format done before AI arrived is a poor use of the technology.

4. **Are you prepared to invest in training staff on how to use the new technology?** It will prove very difficult to fire all existing staff and hire all new staff with more familiarity with AI processes. The best organizations are those that look to up/reskill employees on how to get the full value from ML models.

5. **Are your senior leaders prepared to hand over the reins on the high-stakes decision to implement AI applications?** There is very little room for naysayers when it comes to implementing AI. Steps must be taken to educate senior leaders on the potential and limitations of AI solutions so they will be confident when it comes time to lean on the technology to make certain decisions.

6. **Does your organization have a tolerance for mistakes and setbacks to allow time for the organization and technology to grow together?** Some organizations simply don't tolerate failure in any form. Those organizations are destined to be disappointed

with AI solutions, particularly if they don't work exactly as promised right out of the box. AI is not a plug-and-play technology platform; it requires organizations to evolve and learn how to use them to full advantage.

7. **Does your organization have an executive sponsor with both the expertise and credibility to lead an AI transformation?** This cannot be a case of the blind leading the blind. Your employees want to know that the executive sponsor has intimate familiarity with the technology and can explain precisely what it can and can't do.

8. **Does your organization have the patience for a transformation that can take years to fully accomplish?** Leaders who suffer from a lack of delayed gratification will likely not have the patience to see an AI transformation reach fruition. Patience is not only a virtue in this scenario, it is the lifeblood of AI transformation.

AI and ML models are truly the future of project management. Of this, there is no doubt. The uncertainty, then, is not about whether your organization should embrace AI; it's about whether your organization is willing and ready. These questions can only be answered through a process of unblinking self-assessment. It is time to go forth and ask your organization some tough questions. The payoff could be the ability to be among those leaders adopting AI rather than being left among the laggards.

About the Authors

Antonio Nieto-Rodriguez is the author of the *Harvard Business Review Project Management Handbook*, the featured HBR article *The Project Economy Has Arrived*, and five other books. His research and global impact on modern management have been recognized by Thinkers50. A pioneer and leading authority in teaching and advising executives the art and science of strategy implementation and modern project management, Antonio is a visiting professor in seven leading business schools. He is the founder of Projects&Co and the Strategy Implementation Institute. You can follow Antonio through antonionietorodriguez.com, his LinkedIn newsletter *Lead Projects Successfully*, and online course *Project Management Reinvented for Non-Project Managers*.

Ricardo Viana Vargas, PhD is an experienced leader in global operations, project management, business transformation and crisis management. Founder and managing director of Macrosolutions, a consulting firm with international operations in energy, infrastructure, IT, oil and finance, he managed more than US$20 billion in international projects in the past 25 years. Former chairman of the Project Management Institute (PMI), Ricardo created and led the Brightline® Initiative from 2016 to 2020 and was the director of project management and infrastructure at the United Nations, leading more than 1,000 projects in humanitarian and development projects.

He wrote 16 books in the field, has delivered 250 keynote addresses in 40 countries, and hosts the "5 Minutes Podcast," which has reached 12 million views. Ricardo holds a Ph.D. in Civil Engineering, a master's in Industrial Engineering, and an undergraduate degree in Chemical Engineering.

The Heart of Digital Transformation

SCOTT D. ANTHONY AND PAUL COBBAN

4.

Let's return to 2009. On his first day as DBS Bank's Chief Data and Transformation Officer, co-author Paul Cobban steps into a cab and asks to go to Singapore's leading bank. "Ah," the driver comments, "DBS: damn bloody slow." The driver is referencing the notorious lines that plagued DBS's ATMs at the time. That same year, when preparing to move to Singapore, coauthor Scott Anthony asks for advice about which bank he should use. No one recommends DBS. In fact, customer satisfaction scores at the time ranked DBS fifth … in Singapore.

Fast forward a few years. In 2016, DBS was named the world's best digital bank by *Euromoney*, noting: "It is demonstrably the case that digital innovation pervades every part of DBS" (*Euromoney*, 2016). In 2019, DBS becomes the first bank to simultaneously hold the titles "Bank of the Year" (*The Banker*), "Best Bank in the World" (*Global Finance*), and "World's Best Bank" (*Euromoney*). That year, independent research by Innosight (where Scott works) identified DBS as one of the top 10 business transformations of the past decade.

This sounds like a story of digital transformation, and it is. It's also more than that. DBS's transformation shows how the heart of a digital transformation is, well, a living, breathing human heart. After all, nothing changes unless people's behavior changes.

Successful digital transformation is not about the blind implementation of new technologies; rather, it is the careful application of suitable technology to improve customer solutions. True digital leaders are impatiently curious about what works and what does not. This is a cultural issue, not a strategic issue. Peter Drucker famously noted that culture eats strategy for breakfast. *Digital* culture eats digital strategy for breakfast, lunch, and dinner.

Culture is too often left to executive sloganeering or a part-time hobby for an overstretched HR department. Companies can do better. They must do better. This article describes the culture change at the heart of DBS's transformation and extracts key lessons for leaders looking to address the heart of digital transformation.

DBS's Transformation

The story begins in 2009, when Piyush Gupta took over as CEO. DBS, like many Asian banks, had emerged relatively unscathed from the 2007–2008 global financial crisis. However, it was clear that digitization, cryptocurrency, roboadvisors, and peer-to-peer finance platforms promised significant disruption in the years ahead. Gupta and his team concluded that DBS had to transform.

The pace of technological change meant DBS had to look less like a bank biased toward regulatory compliance and more like a technology company biased toward entrepreneurialism and innovation. It set an aspiration: act like a 28,000-person start-up, which required substantial changes to its technology organization, starting with a decision to insource operations. In 2009, almost all of its operations were outsourced. By the end of 2017, DBS controlled 85% of its operations, allowing it to own its digital transformation more directly. It had also moved two-thirds of its applications to the cloud to provide greater flexibility. In parallel, it changed its organizational structure. Like many banks, historically, DBS separated frontline, market-facing leaders and back-office employees, who primarily worked with third-party vendors, to provide IT solutions. This created a master-and-servant dynamic, in which the front office held the purse strings and prioritized new revenue-generating functionalities over necessary improvements to stability. DBS shifted to a platform operating model that grouped 600 or so applications and their associated teams into 33 platforms, with some aligned to business functions (e.g., lending), others to support functions (e.g., HR, finance), and still others spanning the company (e.g., data and payments). DBS appointed two leaders to each platform: one from business and one from IT. Each platform had a single budget, roadmap, and set of objectives, shared by the joint platform leaders. This change spurred healthy debates about the trade-offs between new functionalities and stability improvements and almost immediately halted the finger-pointing that typically followed an unplanned IT outage.

Nothing Changes Unless People's Behavior Changes

Digital transformation requires that companies upgrade systems, structure in the right way, and invest to ensure people have the right tools and know how to use them. However, those investments only lead to transformation if they are coupled with serious work, helping people adopt and use that technology in meaningfully different ways. Otherwise, you replace fax machines with email, email with Slack, Slack with neurologically transmitted messages (someday!), yet still find past problems perpetuating. As Oracle CEO Safra Catz notes: "The hard thing about these transformations isn't the technology. It's the sociology" (Lindquist, 2016).

Changing habits at scale is tough. Vision statements, knowledge, and logical arguments are not enough. Providing tools, training, and incentives isn't sufficient either. Our experience is that there is a deeper, hidden barrier: institutionalized inertia that borders on an addiction to business as usual.

Successful organizations become successful by repeatedly solving a problem. They grow by solving that problem more effectively and efficiently. Then they develop habits related to how they solve that problem, and the rationale for the habits disappears into unstated assumptions ("That's just the way we do things around here"). Habits are reinforced by standard operating procedures, performance management systems, and operating metrics. The fundamental paradox and the fundamental challenge facing leaders looking to accelerate digital transformation is that the systems that enable success in today's model reinforce behaviors inconsistent with evolving into tomorrow's model. As one executive quipped: "We are organized to deliver predictable, reliable results. And that's exactly the problem."

A visit by a development leader from Netflix highlighted the challenge and opportunity that DBS faced in its digital transformation. The Netflix leader told a story about how another bank had visited Netflix and had bemoaned the fact that Netflix clearly had an advantage in attracting engineers.

"It's easy for you," the bank leader said. "You just cherry-pick young engineers from top U.S. schools. You have access to better talent than we do."

The Netflix leader paused. He asked how old the typical bank engineer was. It turned out, like Netflix, the average bank engineer was about 40 years old, not a fresh-faced university graduate. Then, he noted that Netflix hired many of its engineers from … banks.

"We hire people from banks just like yours," the Netflix leader said. "We just get out of their way."

In other words, the innovators had always been there; it just took something to bring them out. Fortunately, for DBS, it had unintentionally developed a powerful, repeatable tool to do just that.

Hacking Habits with BEANs

In 2016, DBS's top leaders gathered in Singapore to talk about how the bank was progressing. All agreed that, although it had made headway, much work remained. In their discussion, they identified dysfunctional meetings as a major blocker that entrenched organizational inertia and hindered digital transformation. Most meetings at DBS could be charitably described as inefficient. They would often start and run late; sometimes decisions were made, sometimes they were not. People would dutifully arrive at these meetings without a clear sense of why they were going. Some participants were active, but many sat in defensive silence. Meetings, leadership concluded, were suppressing diverse voices and reinforcing the status quo.

To fix those bad habits, DBS introduced a program called MOJO to promote efficient, effective, open, and collaborative meetings. The MO is the meeting owner who is responsible for ensuring that the meeting has a clear agenda, that it starts and ends on time, and that all attendees are given an equal say. The MO also appoints the JO—the joyful observer—to help the meeting run crisply and encourage broad participation. The JO, for example, has the authority to call a "phone Jenga," which requires all attendees to put their phones in a pile on the table. Perhaps most important, at the end of the meeting, the JO holds the MO accountable, providing frank feedback about how things went and how the MO could improve. Even when the JO is a junior-level employee, they are explicitly authorized to be direct with the MO. The presence of an observer and the knowledge that feedback is coming at the end of the meeting nudges the MO to be mindful of meeting behavior.

This approach, supported by physical reminders in meeting rooms (small cards, wall art, and fun paper cubes that can be tossed around in the room) or on video calls (virtual backgrounds), and a range of measurement and tracking tools, have had a powerful impact. Meetings at DBS no longer run late, saving close to 150,000 employee hours per year. Meeting effectiveness, as gauged by ongoing employee surveys, has doubled, and the percentage of employees who feel they have an equal voice in meetings has jumped from 40% to 90%. Improved efficiency and effectiveness don't mean meetings have become dull, however. Living up to their moniker, the JOs have even been known to provide feedback in verse, and legends have spread. During one meeting, the observer bravely told a senior executive who had lost his cool that the blowup had shut down all discussion. The executive welcomed the feedback, promising to do better next time. It's a story that still circulates, reinforcing the behavioral change DBS hoped to drive with MOJO.

Another intervention DBS introduced was a systematic way to encourage empowerment by relaxing unnecessarily constraining policies. DBS set up a special committee named after a self-deprecating Singaporean slang word, *kiasu*, which roughly translates to "behaving in a selfish manner due to fear of missing out." The head of legal and compliance chairs the kiasu committee, which takes the form of a mock courtroom where any employee can "sue" the owner of a policy or process that they feel is getting in the way. The "jury" is made up of some senior executives and some of the most junior-level people in the bank; they collectively deliberate over whether a change should be made. One of the first decisions was to remove the need for physical signatures for approval. The approach caused quite a ripple throughout the company and gave DBS employees confidence that their issues would be heard and addressed.

A 2017–2018 project with Innosight, to create a repeatable "Culture by Design" toolkit, surfaced that the countermeasures DBS had created to address some of its most persistent cultural blockers shared common elements with similar efforts that other companies had used to purposefully shape culture. They all rip a page from the literature on changing habits by purposefully fighting a two-front battle against inertia. They combine a formal behavior enabler (e.g., a checklist or a ritual) and informal artifacts and nudges (e.g., a visual reminder) to drive behavioral change. DBS had learned how to hack habits with BEANs (behavior enablers, artifacts, and nudges), shrinking the challenge of change into microshifts of change.

The crystallization of the BEAN concept allowed DBS to successfully launch a new technology center in Hyderabad (see Anthony et al., 2019), fight against cultural decay triggered by the COVID-19 pandemic, and smartly manage the shift to hybrid work (see Anthony & Cobban, 2021). "Culture change does not come from a wish and a prayer," CEO Gupta reflected. "It can only happen through an orchestrated program that changes and shapes people's behaviors. The BEANs approach is unconventional but, trust me, it works."

Go Deep and Borrow Brilliantly

Creating a successful BEAN starts with being as specific as possible about the problem you are trying to solve. What specific behaviors are you seeking? For DBS, being a 28,000-person start-up meant that it wanted people to be agile, learning oriented, customer obsessed, data driven, and to experiment and take risks. As DBS worked on more specific applications it got even more precise. For example, experimenting and taking risks meant specific behaviors such as "We rapidly test new ideas," "We practice lean experimentation," and "We fail cheap, we fail fast, and we learn even faster." The more specific the behavior, the more you can track and measure whether it is indeed being routinely followed.

Now comes the hard part: going deep to identify what is really blocking one from following desired behaviors. Consider for example, efforts by the Australian arm of King & Woods Mallesons (KWM), a leading law firm, to get its lawyers to adopt digital technologies to aid with common tasks such as document discovery or proofreading.

KWM formed partnerships with key technological vendors, such as Kira, and announced that digitalizing law was a key strategic thrust but that wasn't enough. Why didn't lawyers easily adopt time-saving technology? Maybe the problem was that they didn't know how to use the technology, which could have been solved easily enough with training. That wasn't the real problem. Perhaps it was that lawyers didn't have the discretionary time to invest in training due to a focus on delivering immediate client value, which could have been solved by simplifying or mandating training.

That wasn't the real problem either.

Time is money, which is truer for lawyers than most other professions. For generations, lawyers have broken their day into 6- or 12-minute increments and billed that time to clients at agreed-upon hourly rates. The so-called billable hour model leads to a deeply rooted bias that suggests those who are not billing all available time to clients are underperforming or otherwise not in demand. Further, productivity-improving technology might look like a bad commercial deal to lawyers, as the efficiency gains from using technology lead to a decrease in billable hours. While that can be great for the client, and in fact great for the law firm as the industry shifts to more fixed-fee models, it can feel at least temporarily painful for the lawyer when that has traditionally been the benchmark for their personal achievement.

Understanding the interplay of these subtle issues led to KWM launching several initiatives to support its digital transformation. It decided to let lawyers credit up to 30 hours of legal training against billable-hour targets, making it easier for them to invest in developing new skills. In 2021, KWM lawyers collectively dedicated 7,200 hours to technology training. It also let lawyers receive extra credit in internal billing systems when they use productivity-boosting technology by applying a multiplier to those hours (without increasing billing to clients). For example, a lawyer spending 10 hours using Kira to streamline contract reviews might receive credit for 15 hours of work.

The deeper you go, the more likely you are to find that there is another existing behavior or belief blocking your desired behavior. The more precise you are about this *behavioral blocker*, the greater the odds of developing a high-impact BEAN.

Another key to success is to remember Pablo Picasso's famous maxim: "Good artists copy. Great artists steal." It doesn't matter if your BEAN is original. It just has to work. Consider work we did together to address an issue in Hyderabad, India, DBS's first fully controlled development center. The center opened to much acclaim in 2016. Its design mimicked what you'd see at any hot, young tech venture: open space, snack bars and, of course, the obligatory foosball table. DBS staffed it with developers hand-picked to be entrepreneurial. But when the lights went on, it quickly became clear that employees' day-to-day experiences had little of the start-up feeling DBS sought. The engineers fell into well-worn routines, working methodically and avoiding fast-paced experimentation. Employee engagement significantly lagged behind DBS's aspirations.

After going deep to identify behavioral blockers, we drew inspiration from others to create two high-impact BEANs: Culture Canvas and 70:20:10.

> **Culture Canvas BEAN.** Many developers felt that they jumped into work without discussing its context, so they lacked an understanding of how their project fit with the broader strategy, what was expected of each person working on the project, and so on. The BEAN targeting this blocker was a Culture Canvas inspired by Alexander Osterwalder and Yves Pigneur's canvas, which maps out the key elements of a business model. The Culture Canvas is, likewise, a simple one-page, poster-size template; on it, project teams articulate their business goals and codify team roles and norms. Filling the Culture Canvas out helps teams gain a clearer sense of expectations, organizational context, and who does what. Providing teams with clarity about their goals and the scope to push boundaries further empowers their entrepreneurial spirit. The resulting physical artifact, which includes photos and signatures from members, serves as a visual reminder of the team members' commitments.

> **70:20:10 BEAN.** Developers reported that they lacked time to innovate. The real blocker? Unclear guidance about how to prioritize a seemingly never-ending list of requests. To bust this blocker, we drew inspiration from Google to create the 70:20:10 BEAN, which gives software developers explicit permission to spend 70% of their time on day-to-day work, 20% on work-improvement ideas, and 10% on experiments and pet projects. By formally freeing up chunks of time for unspecified

experimentation, 70:20:10 encourages innovative thinking. A ritual in which developers share what they've learned from their experimental projects with one another helped to reinforce this BEAN.

These BEANs formed the cornerstone of a concerted intervention that helped to boost workers' engagement scores at Hyderabad by 20%. In 2018, LinkedIn named the development center one of the top 25 places to work in India and, in 2019, the bank won a prestigious Zinnov award for being "a great place to innovate."

Eat, Sleep, Innovate (Anthony et al., 2020), the book we coauthored with two of Scott's colleagues from Innosight, contains 101 BEANs designed to encourage behaviors that encourage innovation such as curiosity, collaboration, and experimentation. Visit tiny.cc/101BEANs and steal shamelessly.

We think part of the reason companies have underinvested in culture is that, for the most part, how to develop corporate culture is not taught in business schools and it is not a role modeled by leaders. In other words, it is new for most people. The need has only increased with the increase in virtual and hybrid work. Fortunately, more and more companies see the need, and more and more people are providing a practical playbook for how to go about it (our best answers are in *Eat, Sleep, Innovate*, some of the publications mentioned in this article, and in posts we have been doing on the topic on LinkedIn).

Culture change that sticks and can be scaled is hard but doable. Look again at DBS. It was called "damn bloody slow" in 2009; in 2019, it became the "world's best bank"—a digital transformation but like all digital transformations, one powered by humans. If you are seeking a similar transformation, put your people at the heart of the transformation. Be clear about the specific behaviors you are seeking. Go deep to identify the behavioral blockers standing in the way of success. Develop BEANs to encourage the behaviors, overcome the blockers, and reap the rewards.

References

Anthony, S., Cobban, P., Nair, R., & Painchaud, N. (2019). *Breaking down the barriers to innovation*. Harvard Business Review. https://hbr.org/2019/11/breaking-down-the-barriers-to-innovation

Anthony, S., & Cobban, P. (2021). *3 tactics to accelerate a digital transformation*. Harvard Business Review Online. https://hbr.org/2021/11/3-tactics-to-accelerate-a-digital-transformation

Anthony, S., Cobban, P, Painchaud, N., & Parker, A. (2020). *Eat, sleep, innovate*. Harvard Business Review Press.

Euromoney. (2016). *World's best digital bank 2016: DBS*. Euromoney, https://www.euromoney.com/article/b12kq6p8mv5rh3/world39s-best-digital-bank-2016-dbs

Lindquist, M. (2016). *Oracle's Safra Catz: How finance can lead cloud transformation*. Forbes.com, https://www.forbes.com/sites/oracle/2016/09/20/oracles-safra-catz-how-finance-can-lead-cloud-transformation/?sh=67ce2bce484b

About the Authors

Scott D. Anthony is a Clinical Professor of Strategy & Management at the Tuck School of Business at Dartmouth College and a Managing Director and Managing Partner emeritus at Innosight.

Paul Cobban is the former Chief Data and Transformation for DBS Bank and an advisor, speaker, and writer on culture change.

They are the co-authors (with Natalie Painchaud and Andy Parker) of *Eat, Sleep, Innovate* (Harvard Business Review Press, 2020).

The illustrations on this chapter are by Paul Cobban.

The Digital Transformation Imperative

EMIL ANDERSSON, TAHIROU ASSANE OUMAROU, AND **TONY O'DRISCOLL**

5

The COVID-19 global pandemic was a dramatic accelerant of the application of technology at work. Throughout the world, within a matter of days, millions of people were forced into remote working for the first time. Unable to see each other face-to-face, families worldwide had to quickly master Skype, Zoom, Microsoft Teams, and a host of other virtual collaborative technologies. In April of 2020, just one month after the World Health Organization (WHO) officially declared a COVID-19 pandemic, Zoom's daily users mushroomed to more than 200 million in from a previous maximum total of 10 million (Venturebeat, 2020).

Most organizations were not as fortunate as Zoom. The vast majority of them were grappling with immediate pressing existential concerns. For many, survival was mission number one, and this required them to rethink everything—their purpose, strategy, business model, operating model, employee policies, customers, and how technology factored into the equation across all these dimensions. Whatever the answers to these questions, technology became a major enabler to transform, and the ability to quickly learn and adapt to this new normal was essential to survival.

Meanwhile, technology continues to evolve at breakneck speed, impacting the changing world of work in a myriad of ways. McKinsey's Technology Trends Outlook for 2022 concludes: "Technology continues to be a primary catalyst for change in the world. Technology advances give businesses, governments, and social-sector institutions more possibilities to lift their productivity, invent and reinvent offerings, and contribute to humanity's well-being. And while it remains difficult to predict how technology trends will play out, executives can plan ahead better by tracking the development of new technologies, anticipating how companies might use them, and understanding the factors that affect innovation and adoption" (Chui et al., 2022, p. 1).

Eighty-six percent of the 326 business executives across different functions surveyed by Harvard Business Review Analytic Services in 2021 say their organization had accelerated its digital transformation during the pandemic (Harvard Business Review Analytic Services, 2021). Of the 279 executives who are accelerating their digital transformation efforts, 91% plan to maintain the heightened pace of digital transformation post–COVID-19 or to move even faster—speaking to how significant and sustained they view this shift in the pace of technological change to be. Emerging technologies can be both disruptive and enable businesses seeking to differentiate themselves and create competitive advantage in their endeavors to create value to their customers.

Add to this vibrant ferment of technological evolution a variety of powerful other forces, such as hyper-competitive responses, blurring industry boundaries, residual pandemic effects, volatile geopolitical dynamics, and perpetually shifting customer expectations and the picture becomes highly muddled. To make sense of this bewildering array of transformative forces and fast-evolving new technologies three fundamentals are clear:

First, **turbulence is a fact of organizational life**. Crises are inevitable: A hack that exposes millions of customers' data; a crucial supply chain of raw material used for production is disrupted; a major holiday product launch misses an all-important deadline; a chairman's immediate dismissal for misconduct; or inflation and increased interest rates leading to a major employee layoff. The circumstances of an organization's next major crisis vary, but its appearance is inevitable. Previous Brightline® research surveyed more than 1,200 senior global leaders and executives about management decisions and organizational strengths during and after crisis events (Brightline®, 2018). A total of 68% of our respondents agreed with the inevitability of their organizations facing a crisis in the future. When facing a crisis, organizations must make a deliberate break from their traditional ways of working. Operating in "business-as-usual" mode, prevents organizations from isolating their in-crisis "business unusual" context, identifying new learnings and applying them to post-crisis transformation efforts.

Second, **successful organizations embrace and maximize technology**. Brightline® research shows that organizations that are successful at implementing strategy rank using new technologies as their number one competitive advantage. They see technological breakthroughs, such as artificial intelligence (AI), digital ecosystems, business platforms, metaverse environments and cloud computing, as critical to their success. Yet, technology falls to the number three priority for less successful organizations (Brightline®, 2020a). In the next three years, organizations expect emerging technologies to be a top driver of transformation (Brightline®, 2022). The question (see Figure 1) is: What cutting-edge technologies have the potential for business disruption and how can organizations transform these technologies into enablers that drive business performance in new arenas for growth?

Figure 1. From disrupting to enabling.

Third, **organizations need to better lead and manage the transformation journey**. According to Brightline® research, 70% of enterprise transformation projects fail to meet business leaders' expectations (Brightline®, 2022). The depth, scope, and complexity of enterprise transformations reveal why this failure rate is so high. Their primary objectives continuously evolve. They are inherently multifaceted. They are simultaneously far-reaching in vision and pragmatic in execution. They are flexible and schedule-driven, value-focused, and explorative. They affect the activities of a single worker in a single department and the operations of entire business ecosystems.

According to Brightline® research (Brightline®, 2022), ways of working and increased transformation capabilities top the list of expected transformation outcomes. Participants in our research highlight the importance of increased organizational agility and adaptability, ability to catalyze innovation, increased resiliency to externalities, and dexterity to adopt to digital and technological changes. These are all elements of successful digital transformation.

Challenges Facing Digital Transformation

Identifying something as critically important to the sustainability of the enterprise as the need to improve the success rate of digital transformation efforts does not necessarily mean the problem has been solved. It has merely been identified. If digital transformation is at the top of leaders' agendas, we need to quickly learn some fundamental lessons if it is to be successfully put into practice. As we have seen, there is an abundance of research suggesting that organizations repeatedly struggle with converting digital transformation from idea to reality. Project Management Institute (PMI) identified the cost of failed transformation efforts across the globe in 2020 at US$2 trillion. This cost is the equivalent of the GDP of Brazil at a macro scale, or US$3 million per minute at a micro scale (Brightline® 2020b).

There are a host of explanations as to why this happens. Mike Sutcliff, Raghav Narsalay, and Aarohi Sen identified two main reasons why digital transformations hit the corporate buffers: unspoken disagreement among top managers about goals and a divide between the digital capabilities supporting the pilot and the capabilities available to support scaling it (Sutcliff et al., 2019). Our own work at Brightline® research suggests that the route to successfully implementing digital transformation requires four key elements, elaborated on in the following sections.

Framing the Transformation

A fundamental issue is that there is often a lack of agreement as to what digital transformation actually is. At the very basic level, digital transformation can be thought of as technology used to improve customer value and experience through innovating business models and developing and enabling the people and processes of the organization.

Research by GetSmarter looked at different interpretations of the term digital transformation (GetSmarter, 2022). "Digital transformation in business has historically been defined as using technologies to create new—or optimize existing—processes, culture, and customer experiences. Technology is implemented to meet changing business and market needs, and to take a company into the digital future. Its adoption impacts the entire organization and requires revolutionary thinking and action," it notes before adding, "Perhaps because of its far-reaching influence on companies, industries, and roles, digital transformation has gathered many different interpretations over time." Its research found that digital transformation means different things to different people and identified 20 definitions—ranging from "the incorporation of digital technology in every domain of the business" to "creative disruption" by way of "change in an organization's business model" and "sustainable innovation."

Shared understanding feeds into a shared sense of purpose. Any transformation needs to have a widely shared sense of purpose and a clearly articulated set of objectives to achieve that purpose. Accordingly, the organization, the leaders, and the employees need to have an answer to this fundamental question: Why are we transforming?

In addition to identifying and agreeing on the purpose, it's important to map and scope what the transformation actually entails. Regardless of digital or not, at Brightline® we believe there are four main types of transformation for organizations to consider (see Figure 2):

Maintain. The objective is to maintain core businesses by improving efficiency in operations, support, and processes. This can be in the form of increasing sales to customers with the same offers or reducing costs by digitizing or automating processes.

Improve. The objective is to improve core business value perception by reengineering existing processes. For example, the organization aims to expand sales by developing better delivery systems for customers.

Extend. The objective is to increase core business value by extending into new yet adjacent business arenas. That could be selling existing offerings to new customer segments in a given geography or expanding into new geographies.

Reimagine. The objective is to reinvent the business by developing new models of value differentiation and delivery. This can be in the form of changing industry structure through acquisitions/alliances or developing new arenas for growth via ecosystem partnerships.

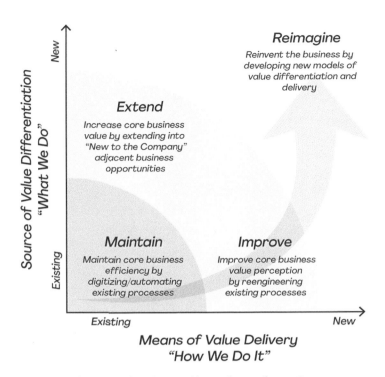

Figure 2. The what and how of transformation.

Once the type of digital transformation is established, the next step is to enable this vision with technology. Yet, the main challenge with digital transformation does not lie with the technology itself but rather with the adoption and application of the new technology or process by the people in the organization. Our work at Brightline® has led us to develop the Brightline® Transformation Compass (BTC). This is built on the realization that the key to a successful transformation is building a movement that aligns inside-out and outside-in approaches. A transformation shaped by BTC is led by committed senior leaders inside your organization and authored and driven by large numbers of your own employees—the management and frontline team members who have a stake in your success.

Creating the Role of CTO

Managing these dynamic and divergent forces requires a versatile leader. The role of chief transformation officer (CTO) is increasingly recognized as an important element in achieving digital transformation (Brightline®, 2022). This individual must be able to understand and respect diverse stakeholder points of view and yet align all parties in pursuit of greater goals. To do so, the CTO must also be able to build trust in the process, so that stakeholders engage as owners and work to collaboratively drive change, rather than feeling that change is happening to them. Ultimately, the transformation leader must be able to mobilize the power that lies at the intersection of technology and human creativity, complexity, passion, and energy to build a permanent, company-wide changing capability.

Powering People Plus Technology

The crucial realization must be that digital transformation—now more than ever—requires organizations and leaders to put people first. Technology does not change organizations, people do. People literally breathe life into every organization. People make the organization stop or go. They are the strategy in motion. Without the ongoing engagement of people in driving the transformation effort, it is doomed to failure.

Organizations mastering digital transformation understand that change efforts are not primarily about the technology itself. Technology is an enabler rather than the answer itself; it is about adoption of technologies and how technologies enable the organization to find other ways to deliver value.

In their work looking at why some digital transformation efforts succeed and others fail, Behnam Tabrizi, Ed Lam, Kirk Girard, and Vernon Irvin simply conclude that "digital transformation is not about technology" (Tabrizi et al., 2019). "Most digital technologies provide possibilities for efficiency gains and customer intimacy. But if people lack the right mindset to change and the current organizational practices are flawed, digital transformation will simply magnify those flaws," they say and go on to recommend that leaders reconnect with the fundamentals to focus "on changing the mindset of [an organization's] members as well as the organizational culture and processes before they decide what digital tools to use and how to use them. What the members envision to be the future of the organization drove the technology, not the other way around."

If digital transformation is personal, organizations need to do a lot of work to harness the discretionary effort of its people to maximize the power of technology to successfully transform their organization. This is about creating processes and developing skills, that enable people to understand and best utilize technology. When it comes to digital transformation, organizations are often castigated for their lack of progress; however, it is worth noting that at an individual level, there is also a lot of work to do. In 2019, Michael Netzley and Robin Speculand created the Digital Maturity Index (DMI) to identify an individual's position on their digital journey. The catalyst was the urgent need to understand an individual's ability to learn and adopt digital technologies and methodologies. Additionally, significant individual differences in digital maturity were becoming apparent, which were further complicating digital transformation. The DMI assesses an individual's position along their own digital journey (not within their organization), provides recommendations for improvement, and identifies equally their knowing and doing skills and categorizes the findings into three stages: reacting, embedding, and strategizing. The 2022 results (from a sample of 1,463 respondents) revealed that individuals have more knowledge than skills to participate in digital transformation. As a result, they are struggling to move from acquiring new knowledge to embedding it into practice. Netzley and Speculand call this difference the Digital Knowing-Doing Gap. Their latest survey suggests that a massive 71% of people are in the reacting category of response, 24% in embedding the response, and a mere 5% in the strategizing response (Netzley & Speculand, 2022).

This DMI research demonstrates that training and development are vital. The question of how to close the technology gaps is often challenging. Many of the organizations that need new technology often do not have the necessary know-how and skills to successfully implement it—this also applies to culture. New technologies often require in-depth expertise, which takes time to develop. The more complex the technology solution, the more likely it is that external resources, rather than internal resources, will best bring sought-after capabilities and know-how. A Brightline® study shows that the involvement of a trusted and experienced external partner can play a pivotal role in the curation and adoption of the kinds of emerging technologies that power an enterprise transformation (Brightline®, 2020a). While external sourcing is the quickest way to a digitally enabled organization, changes in mindset, leadership, and general upskilling are required within the organization to sustain the change effort.

Powering the Customer Experience

The people in the organization and the organization's customers are the leading forces in any digital transformation. A senior vice president in the transformation and finance department in a large telecommunications company told us: "[Transformation value] starts from the customer's perspective. What are the pain points for the customer? How do they want to do business with [us]? You start there and say, 'how do we go fix these things?' Usually, if you can go fix some of those things it's because of inefficient processes, old ways of doing things. If you fundamentally improve that customer experience, there's value that comes out the back side of it, whether it's retaining your customers longer, selling more to them, or actually making your teams more productive and more efficient" (Brightline®, 2022, p. 7).

According to Brightline® research, evolving customer expectations was considered a top driver for enterprise transformation in 2022 (Brightline®, 2022). Similarly, customer experience scores high for expected outcome and success criteria in enterprise transformation. While it is hardly surprising that customer experience tops the list vis-à-vis transformation drivers, expected outcome, and success criteria, it speaks volumes for our belief that customer insights are crucial for the success of a transformation initiative. Yet, how many digital transformations have delivered transformative customer experiences? Not many. Relentless customer focus is what still separates the corporate greats from the mediocre. Witness Amazon.

It is easy to be daunted by the forces at work, but the fundamentals of organizational and business life remain as true as ever. People. Processes. Customers. Organizations undertaking enterprise transformation with digital technologies would do well to consider two basic notions: (1) what we do, which can also be expressed as the source of value differentiation and can fall anywhere between existing and new; and (2) how we do it—this is the means of value delivery, which can also fall between existing and new. Challenge your organization with these two simple notions to ignite your digital transformation.

References

Brightline®. (2018). *Learning from crisis mode.* https://www.brightline.org/resources/learning-from-crisis-mode/

Brightline®. (2020a). Strategic transformation research. https://www.brightline.org/resources/strategic-transformation-research/

Brightline®. (2020b). New executive report on how leaders succeed at strategic transformation in transformative times. https://www.brightline.org/press/releases/new-executive-report-on-how-leaders-succeed-at-strategic-transformation-in-transformative-times/

Brightline®. (2022). *The chief transformation officer.* https://www.brightline.org/resources/the-chief-transformation-officer/

Chui, M., Roberts, R., & Yee, L. (2022). *Technology trends outlook 2022 McKinsey & Co.* https://www.mckinsey.com/business-functions/mckinsey-digital/our-insights/the-top-trends-in-tech?cid=other-soc-lkn-mip-mck-oth---&sid=7535201541&linkId=180857839)

GetSmarter. (2022). *What digital transformation means and how it impacts you.* https://www.getsmarter.com/blog/career-advice/what-digital-transformation-means-and-how-it-impacts-you/

Harvard Business Review Analytic Services. (2021). *Digital acceleration redefines the future of work.* https://hbr.org/sponsored/2021/09/data-strategy-the-missing-link-in-artificial-intelligence-enabled-transformation

Netzley, M., & Speculand, R. (2022). *Digital maturity index report.* Bridges Business Consultancy, 2022.

Sutcliff, M., Narsalay, R., & Sen, A. (2019). *The two big reasons that digital transformations fail.* HBR.org. https://hbr.org/2019/10/the-two-big-reasons-that-digital-transformations-fail

Tabrizi, B., Lam, E., Girard, K., & Irvin, V. (2019). *Digital transformation is not about technology.* HBR.org. https://hbr.org/2019/03/digital-transformation-is-not-about-technology

Venturebeat.com. (2020). *Zoom's daily participants jumped from 10 million to over 200 million in 3 months.* https://venturebeat.com/business/zooms-daily-active-users-jumped-from-10-million-to-over-200-million-in-3-months/

Zobell, S. (2018). *Why digital transformation fails: Closing the $900 billion hole in enterprise strategy.* Forbes.com. https://www.forbes.com/sites/forbestechcouncil/2018/03/13/why-digital-transformations-fail-closing-the-900-billion-hole-in-enterprise-strategy/?sh=141855277b8b

About the Authors

Emil Andersson, MSc, is a strategy research consultant at Brightline®, a Project Management Institute (PMI) initiative. He is a practitioner in the field of business strategy, transformation, and project management. Emil has been involved in over 40 global strategic projects and has a strong interest in disruptive technologies and how organizations create and deliver value.

Tahirou Assane Oumarou, MASc, P.Eng., PMP is director of Brightline®, a Project Management Institute (PMI) initiative. He has over 20 years of experience in leadership roles, civil engineering, strategy, transformation, and project management. Previously, he worked as the deputy director of the infrastructure and project management group in the United Nations Office for Project Services supporting the successful implementation of peace-building, humanitarian, and development projects around the world. He was also a senior project manager with the Ministry of Transportation in Ontario.

Tony O'Driscoll, Ed.D. is an adjunct professor at Duke University's Fuqua School of Business and Pratt School of Engineering and serves as a Research Fellow at Duke Corporate Education. These appointments afford Tony the unique opportunity to apply cutting-edge academic research to address increasingly complex business challenges. Dr. O'Driscoll's current research and practice examines how rapidly emerging technologies are disrupting existing industry structures and business models. He specifically focuses on how to develop leadership systems that enable organizations to adapt and evolve in increasingly unpredictable and turbulent business environments. His new book, *Everyday Superhero*, explores how you can inspire everyone to create real change at work. You can follow Dr. O'Driscoll's work at tonyodriscoll.com.

Pipelines to Platforms to Protocols: Reconfiguring Value and Redesigning Markets

SANGEET PAUL CHOUDARY

From the compass to the printing press, the steam engine to the electric lightbulb, economic history shows that whenever technology disrupts the market forces of production and consumption, value creation will change in step. The level to which individual players benefit from these technological gains is then dictated by the degree of market power they wield.

Over the past decade, my work has focused on the shift from pipelines to platforms as a transformative shift in value creation that shaped the first two decades of the 21st century. I believe that the shift from pipelines to platforms, now widely accepted, will shift further with the emergence of protocols as the foundational technology of Web3.

This, I believe, is the real shift of our time—a fundamental redesign in value creation and markets, not just a shift toward decentralization or read/write/own, as many of the Web1 to Web2 to Web3 proponents often claim.

This article explains why this transition matters and is becoming increasingly inevitable.

The Rise of Pipelines

Value creation in the industrial era was dominated by pipelines. Pipelines are the traditional industrial business model, characterized by a linear, unidirectional flow of value from producer to consumer, where value is created by the producer and shipped out to the customer, who then pays for the value. It was the technology of the industrial era that shaped the pipeline model of value creation throughout much of the 20th century.

First, **technologies enabling mass production**—assembly lines optimized through factory automation, backed by large-scale, organization management—allowed us to aggregate production at scale. Together, these gave us the tools of mass production and gave birth to large corporations, particularly during the post–World War II geopolitical shift toward globalization.

On the consumption side, **the rise of mass media**—from newspapers to radio and then television —provided the means for influencing consumption at scale like never before. The rise of cities and suburban populations provided the market conditions for mass consumption to meet mass production through retail, forcing prices down and improving choice and convenience.

Finally, **the shift to globalization and international trade**—spurred further by standardization technologies, particularly container shipping—led to the creation of global supply chains, connecting mass production with mass consumption globally.

By perfecting the technologies of mass production, mass consumption, and global connectivity, the industrial era perfected its ability to scale value creation through the pipeline model and benefit from supply-side economies of scale.

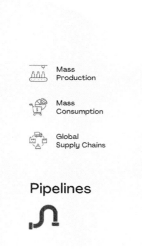

Pipelines

Figure 1. Pipelines

The Shift to Platforms

Throughout history, technological shifts and market forces have worked together to drive new paradigms for value creation. With the rise of the internet and digital technologies, this combination of technological changes and market forces drove the shift from pipelines to platforms.

First, **the tools of production could now be distributed**, rather than centralized. Consider the news industry as an example. To create and distribute news at scale, you had to be a large newspaper company, but then the internet decentralized the tools of publishing and distribution, so that anybody with access to wiki or web-authoring tools could produce and disseminate news.

Second, the capture of data at scale—for instance, through social technologies and subsequently through connected devices—combined with improvements in machine learning (ML) and artificial intelligence (AI) drove **the rise of personalized consumption.**

As markets shifted from mass production and mass consumption to distributed production and personalized consumption, the internet provided a **global connectivity infrastructure** to connect the two. Mobile-based connectivity and cloud computing enabled the creation of a new alternative for global value exchange. Cloud hosting connected distributed production to personalized consumption through a global network. Together, these three technologies drove the rise of platforms as the dominant model of value creation. Platforms connected producers and consumers with each other, allowing them to create an exchange value and facilitating these interactions at scale. By adding more and more producers to these platforms, there was more choice for consumers, enabling these platforms to benefit from demand-side economies of scale.

Platforms rearchitected value creation away from *mass production connected to mass consumption* to *distributed production connected to personalized consumption*. By aggregating fragmented markets, platforms reduced search costs—the costs incurred in counterparty discovery. By standardizing transactions at scale, platforms reduced bargaining costs—the costs incurred in negotiating the terms of exchange. Additionally, by acting as central intermediaries with market-wide data capture and visibility, platforms reduced verification and policing costs—the costs incurred in imputing trust to transactions by verifying and policing those transactions.

In achieving the above, platforms created massive value while also gaining inordinate market power. Demand-side economies of scale—manifested through network effects and learning effects —coalesced entire markets around a few dominant platforms.

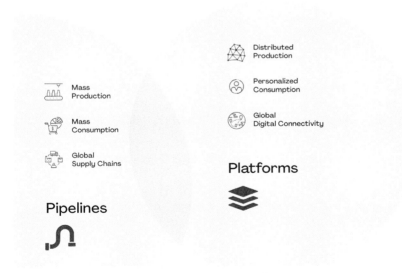

Figure 2. Platforms

The Resurgence of Protocols

Protocols—more specifically, permission-less blockchain protocols—provide a new organizing and governance mechanism to organize actors in an ecosystem. Unlike platforms, protocols neither provide end-to-end market infrastructure nor do they internalize transaction policing and verification. Since protocols do not themselves provide market infrastructure or internalize transaction policing and verification, they need to set up the economic incentives for other ecosystem actors to provision these services. They achieve this by issuing tokens to reward desirable actions in the ecosystem. As the value of market activity in the ecosystem increases, the value of the token—tied to protocol usage—increases as well.

Just as there was a fundamental shift in value configuration from pipelines to platforms, so are production, consumption, and markets poised to transform again with the shift from platforms to protocols. Protocols have often been dismissed by Web3 skeptics as hacker tools that will only impact a small community. Instead, protocols—in combination with tokens—look increasingly likely to power the next generation of market economics.

First, **protocols (in combination with tokens) change the incentives and returns on production**. The platform economy has often been criticized for skewing rewards away from external producers, who commit resources to the platform and incur risks, and centralizing rewards with the central platform organization. Token rewards provide an alternate incentive mechanism where ecosystem producers are incentivized for desirable actions that grow market activity. These tokens, in turn, grow in value as overall market activity increases, enabling external producers to benefit from returns.

In addition to improving returns on production, protocols—particularly, through non-fungible tokens (NFTs)—also empower producers by establishing, transferring, and enforcing property rights over the assets they produce. Well-structured token incentives, combined with the verifiability of asset ownership, skew rewards of production back to the producer.

On the consumption side, **protocols disentangle consumers from the lock-in enforced by platforms**. Platforms drove market efficiencies by leveraging data to reduce search costs and verification costs. This involved an inherent trade-off as market participants—particularly consumers—needed to surrender their data to the platform to benefit from these market efficiencies. This surrender of data and attendant lock-in increased the risks of privacy invasion, loss of agency through overdependence, and unilateral censorship, as centralized platforms could change their policies at will.

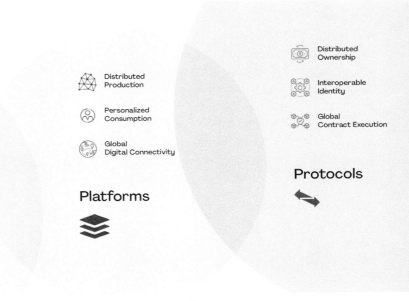

Figure 3. Protocols

Blockchain protocols **reduce transaction verification costs without absorbing these costs as intermediaries,** instead allowing market actors to verify transactions and enforce contracts while preserving data privacy. Since identity and data no longer need to be locked into a platform to verify and impute trust to transactions, consumer identity now becomes interoperable, and consumers can participate across multiple platforms and protocols while retaining custodianship over their identity.

Protocols bring decentralized ownership, giving creators greater control over what they're creating. Alongside distributed production and market access on their own terms, creators will have the property rights to leverage as they choose. Production can be scaled up even further, especially in markets where ownership of intellectual property is valuable to the creator.

With protocols, property rights go back to the creator and identity goes back to the consumer. However, much like pipelines needed standards in global supply chains and platforms needed a global compute infrastructure, protocols require a new operating infrastructure to manage decentralized transaction execution at scale. **Global contract execution,** therefore, becomes very important. The rise of blockchain and distributed ledgers provides a shared view of the history of transactions: who owns what and when. Smart contracts give a shared infrastructure for executing these at scale. Again, technology brings changes in production and consumption, together creating a new mechanism for managing market activity.

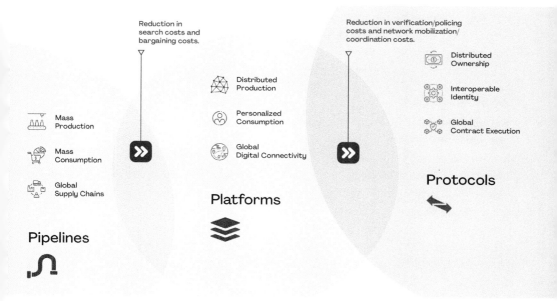

Figure 4. From pipelines to platforms to protocols

What's Next?

While it's now undisputed that there was a significant shift from pipelines to platforms, I believe we are now in the early stages of a similar shift from platforms to protocols. Much like the arrival of platforms didn't signal the end of pipelines, the emergence of protocols will not end the era of platforms. Instead, pipelines, platforms, and protocols will coexist as different mechanisms to organize and configure value in the economy. Some parts of the economy will be best managed through platforms, whereas other use cases will lend themselves to decentralized protocol-based management.

In the last two years, we have seen a number of tipping points that will herald the arrival of protocols. Two factors in particular—the need for interoperability and the attractiveness of new reward-sharing mechanisms— will be key determiners of the speed of this shift. Decentralized finance and the rise of tokens now provide the financial machinery for new reward-sharing mechanisms. Similarly, the need for greater interoperability in the design of virtual worlds is another factor that could spur the adoption of protocols.

Finally, for all the talk about decentralization, this shift is less about equity and more about value. We will undoubtedly see the major platforms, with their advantage of scale, leverage this new set of technologies in a way that best reinforces their current economics. Facebook (now Meta), after experimenting with Libra, is now investing heavily in protocols more broadly. **It would be naive to assume that protocols themselves will also not attract new modes of value capture and control**. We're still in the early stages of a massive shift. One thing remains certain—the new value will be created, configured, and captured differently from the old.

About the Author

Sangeet Paul Choudary is the founder of Platformation Labs and the coauthor of *Platform Revolution* and *Platform Scale*. He has advised the leadership of more than 40 of the Fortune 500 firms and has been selected as a Young Global Leader by the World Economic Forum. Sangeet's work on platforms has been selected by *Harvard Business Review* as one of the top 10 ideas in strategy and has been featured thrice in the HBR Top 10 Must Reads compilations. Sangeet is a frequent keynote speaker at leading global forums, including the G20 Summit, the World50 Summit, the United Nations, and the World Economic Forum.

Securing Innovation and Antifragility as Part of Your Digital Transformation Strategy

VINCENZO CORVELLO AND ANNIKA STEIBER

"We want to be fire, wish for the wind."
(Taleb, 2013, p. 2)

7

Crises, such as the COVID-19 pandemic and the war in Ukraine, are still perceived as rare events. If we consider large-scale disastrous events in general, however, we can no longer consider them exceptional. If we look at the disastrous global or regional events that have occurred over the past 50 years, we will realize that a conservative estimate is that, on average, we have one disastrous event every fourth year. Among these, we can count events such as the attack on the Twin Towers on 11 September 2001, the Iraq War in 2003, the 2008 financial crisis, and the debt crises in Argentina and Greece. And, obviously, the COVID-19 pandemic should be added to this list.

These large-scale shocks have been referred to as *black swans* (Taleb, 2013). If black swans show up with this frequency, they represent normality, which is why managers in any digital transformations of their businesses need to build, buy, or in other ways secure strategic capabilities to manage their firms in the event of new black swans.

Black swans' impact on the economy and society is commonly devastating. What is less often noted is that they also change the business context in which individuals and organizations operate. In the business world, these events change the very conditions for competition, hence also generating opportunities for companies.

Recently, the management literature has focused on the concept of resilience, that is, *the capability of resisting shocks*. However, of more interest for the business community is the capability of exploiting crises as new business opportunities, something commonly referred to as *antifragility*, which is the focus of this article.

From Resilience to Antifragility

An organization is fragile when, in facing a shock, it collapses and ceases to exist or its performance dramatically deteriorates. A resilient organization, on the other hand, can survive the shock. The literature highlights various nuances of the concept of resilience. There is *passive resilience*, sometimes referred to as *robustness*, which refers to when companies absorb shocks and then return to initial operating conditions. This type of resilience is not suitable for situations of greater change in which, after the shock, the system does not return to its initial conditions. What we then need is *transformative resilience*, that is, when an organization not only manages to survive the shock but change and adapt to the new context.

Antifragility, on the other hand is of a different nature. The change in the context now creates opportunities for competitive advantage. Antifragile organizations try to identify these opportunities before their competitors and quickly change their business model to accommodate them. In this way, they manage to occupy a better position.

Innovation in the Post–COVID-19 Era

Innovation naturally plays a central role in an antifragile organization. If the context changes, it is natural that businesses must develop new products and processes to adapt. However, innovation cannot only be the result of long-term research and development processes conducted in laboratories of large companies. Instead, innovation also needs to be the result of cocreation with different players in the corporation's ecosystem. One specifically interesting category of partners is *high-tech start-ups*. These intrinsically entrepreneurial companies can manage the short-term adaptation required by the changes brought about by black swans.

A start-up could be viewed as a business experiment facing high uncertainty. A start-up, therefore, is by nature flexible, entrepreneurial, and fluid; it is not restricted by established routines, consolidated investments, or rigid mental schemes; on the contrary, it is often made up of small groups of people, very cohesive, with an entrepreneurial attitude, and ready to question their own assumptions. All these features make start-ups a powerful strategic avenue for larger firms to explore new contexts. By supporting promising start-ups, a larger firm can therefore not only resist crises, it can improve its performance and become antifragile.

Building Antifragility with Start-Ups

To build antifragile larger firms with start-ups, large firms first need to answer the question: How do we design such a system?

The design of the system needs to fulfill two requirements:

1. When large companies leverage on start-ups, the system must become antifragile.
2. There must be a win-win for both start-ups and larger firms.

Large corporations are established players and can provide resources and management and market knowledge to start-ups. Start-ups, on the other hand, commonly have access to new emerging technological ecosystems and intellectual capital in the forms of a talented, knowledgeable, and a motivated team, and/or, in many cases, also patents.

When a system with large and small firms is built on trust, a win-win strategy, includes instruments for an effective and efficient collaboration, and a joint mindset focused on a constant evolution of new value creation for users, the system can become antifragile.

The Haier case (described by Dr. Steiber in her book *Leadership for a Digital World*) is a great illustration of a successful and antifragile system consisting of Haier, other large firms, and tech start-ups. In 2000, Haier started their digital transformation journey, shortly after the chairman and CEO had attended the World Economic Forum and realized that internet technology will disrupt the hardware business. Part of the company's digital transformation was the development of ecosystems, a requirement to survive in the fourth industrial revolution. Haier's transformation into an ecosystem company demanded a clear strategic focus on what to focus on, be best at, and in what areas to collaborate with other players. Another requirement was that the ecosystem was to provide both efficiency at scale and learning at scale. The ecosystems were built around user experiences, enabled by networking capabilities, and they generate income through value-added sharing among all participants who gravitate around users' needs. To effectively coordinate all players' activities in the value chain, contracts are made among the players. The contract is not a typical procurement relationship, but an agreement for cocreation among parties in which they all focus on user needs and share value created. Finally, the contract is an *infinite contract* with the purpose of continuing the game. To create the best user experience, the ecosystem can expand with new players and, as user needs keep changing, the game continues.

Conclusion and Managerial Impact

The crisis generated by the COVID-19 pandemic has changed our way of viewing the evolution of social, economic, and technological systems. This is no longer a linear development, but instead a discontinuous development interspersed with crises that require continuous adaptations.

Collaboration with start-ups in systems, or ecosystems, can be a winning strategy for larger firms to not only quickly adapt but also to prosper and develop new business opportunities arising from disruptive changes. For these systems to be antifragile, they need to be designed based on a win-win mentality, complementing skills and competencies, as well as mechanisms that secure a self-evolving system.

References

Taleb, N. N. (2012). *Antifragile: Things that gain from disorder*. Random House.

Steiber, A. (2022). *Leadership for a digital world*. Springer.

About the Authors

Dr. Vincenzo Corvello is an associate professor in the Department of Engineering, University of Messina. He holds a PhD in Business and Economic Engineering from the University Federico II of Naples. His research interests are in the fields of entrepreneurship, innovation management, and antifragility. He is cofounder and former CEO of Beautiful Mind, an academic spin-off from the University of Calabria. He is a Research Associate at the London School of Economics and Political Science, London Multimedia Lab. His research has been supported by national and international research grants and he is editor-in-chief of the *European Journal of Innovation Management*.

Dr. Annika Steiber has over three decades of experience from research on management innovations and she has held executive positions in high-growth firms. She is a professor, executive, speaker, investor, and the founder and director of the Rendanheyi Silicon Valley Center. She is the author of 10 management books on the theme of management for a digital age, including *The Google Model: Management for Continuous Innovation in a Rapidly Changing World*, *The Silicon Valley Model: Management for Entrepreneurship*, *Management in a Digital Age: Will China Surpass Silicon Valley?*, and *Leadership for a Digital World: The Transformation of GE Appliances*.

The Rendanheyi Silicon Valley Center was founded in 2020, in California, in collaboration with the Haier Model Institute (HMI). HMI focuses on management for the 21st century with a mission of supporting forward-looking business leaders in managing their companies for long-term survival in a digital, fast-moving age by offering a new generation of business webinars and certificate courses. For more information, please contact Dr. Annika Steiber at annika.steiber@gmail.com.

How Established Companies Can Surf New Tech Waves

ELISA FARRI AND FABIO VERONESE

Starting in the 2010s, the accelerated speed of technology changes has offered immense opportunities for companies across industries. Significant technological and digital advances—from Internet of Things (IoT), artificial intelligence (AI) and machine learning (ML), to quantum computing—have enabled new strategies, business models, and operating models. The most successful companies in unlocking value from new technologies have been digital natives and this is no coincidence. Born online, their DNA is tech and data ready. For them, digital transformation is a current, natural state, not an ambitious *vision* to achieve.

It's therefore no surprise that many traditional, non-tech companies strive to navigate new technological environments, and even when they (dare to) embrace the latest technology, their investment often fails to pay off. The main reason why established companies find it hard to unlock real value from new technology is the illusion that innovation and experimentation can be bought and delegated to suppliers or tech partners—without a direct investment in developing internal capabilities. The typical approach is what we call *wait and react*. Some companies wait for a pioneer to run a successful experiment with a new technology, then ask their suppliers to simply copy and apply it to a similar internal use case. Others wait for their technological partner or supplier to recommend general off-the-shelf offerings. Whereas others, more skeptical, wait longer for a technology to be widely employed in their industry before they even start considering it as an option.

Over the past decade, some companies have understood the limits and difficulties of the *wait and react* approach and have tried to be more *proactive*, scouting and testing new emerging technologies. One common approach to being more proactive has been the setup of hotspots, accelerators, tech incubators, and scout teams. Distinct teams pilot the radar system to see what's ahead. Based on internal briefs, they identify new technology to address business opportunities with a craving for major use cases or applications to find a supportive sponsor or stakeholder on the business side, willing to experiment.

While this alternative approach can help in understanding how the world is changing, it fails in building a widespread internal capability to experiment and scale up new technology effectively. Our experience shows that this approach has indeed two main critical downsides.

First, there are proven difficulties in integrating a new technology piloted by a peripheral team into the wider legacy organization. This is also true for more near-term technologies that already have a clear commercial application but require employees to acquire new skills or for the organization to rethink some aspects of the current operating model.

Second, new technology, digital services, or apps are often not adopted as expected (or at all) because they are perceived as too distant from the core activities of the business. Typically, small tech teams spend more time scouting than they do sharing the output of what they do with others in the organization. It is hard to drive commitment without structured and extensive communication about new technological changes. Furthermore, preparing the organization for change requires understanding the people and organizational challenges embedded in the new technological changes; this is an activity that most peripheral teams do not undertake because it's considered part of the corporate change management process.

So, what can executives do to navigate the complexities of technology scouting, adoption, and integration in legacy organizations?

With so much to gain from new technology, it's a shame to let opportunities slip by because of the wrong approach. The following sections describe what we have learned by observing and working with large, established companies who want to be in control of their decisions about new technology, rather than passively waiting and reacting like followers.

Do Not Delegate to the Periphery

The word *curate* originates from the Latin word *curare*, which means "to take care of." Traditionally, curators are content specialists who find and select artwork around a specific theme, document and conduct original research, and share the results through exhibitions or publications.

Curators do not delegate. They do it themselves. Similarly, managers should invest their time and efforts in a continuous hunt. Curious about what's going on in new tech trends, they should be fearlessly open to being exposed to progress. Guided by their judgment of the novelty and relevance of new technology for their business and organization, executives should not delegate to others (be their partner or supplier) decisions about what to experiment with and what not to. With intellectual humility, they should not be afraid to admit that they don't know something. When they sense something should be of interest, they should share it broadly with the rest of the organization and support early-stage discoveries, especially when benefits are not yet clear.

By drawing on the curation process of museums, executives can develop a more effective practice to proactively explore, select, and purpose new emerging technologies with intention. Rather than delegating to separate peripheral teams (internal or external), a curation approach ensures:

A better fit with the core of the organization's activities. It goes beyond connecting new technology to business needs and market readiness. It requires looking at new technology from a holistic view that encompasses the wider organization: people, processes, technology, and systems.

A broader and structured sharing. It goes beyond the elite circle of tech scouts. It reaches out to wider audiences, making data and information about new technology accessible to larger groups, eventually reaching all employees.

Focus on Learning, Not on Immediate Applicability

Every time a new technology arrives on the scene, executives struggle with the same question: Where can we apply it first? Instead of looking for major use cases or applications to demonstrate a more compelling value proposition or business case (which is rarely the case—as emerging technologies do not match the needs of today, rather those of tomorrow), executives should frame their goals in terms of learning quickly, cheaply, and simply.

Successful companies are those that get smart about new technology faster than the competition. They research, discuss with experts and pioneers, and progressively get their hands dirty with small experiments. As they become more familiar with new technology, they refine their opinions, become more confident, and ultimately make better decisions (i.e., on the most impactful problems that a new technology can tackle) independently of others.

In today's age of perpetual transformation, acquiring complete knowledge about new technology should not be approached as a one-and-done exercise. Avoid falling into the trap of flipping through a benchmarking study that gives a false sense of security. Executives should make it part of their routine and, more importantly, have fun (not fear) with early exposure to new technology. Rather than waiting for a tech partner or vendor to pitch a new application or use case, they should invest time in reading about new technology, attending tech fairs, sitting in on keynotes, experiencing demos, and talking to early adopters. The more frequent the exposure to information, the faster they learn, and the more effective they will become at exercising good judgment.

Build Your Own Portfolio of Experiments

Although an experimental mindset permeates much of the tech sector, it is still common to find executives discussing whether or not an emerging technology will lead to more revenues or improved customer experience.

Why debate this point if companies can simply run an experiment to find out more about it?

Tech companies are champions in complementing judgment with experiment-based insights. They run experiments continuously, eager to discover and understand more about how a new technology works. Tech champions run up to hundreds or thousands of tests yearly, compared to the few dozen run by traditional companies.

There are two common pitfalls made by incumbents. First, they believe that one big experiment can answer all the questions. Experimentation is a muscle to train every day. It takes an organized portfolio of small, sequenced experiments to build a widespread capability to systematically embed learnings into decisions. Second, experimentation is no game for solo players. There is a common belief that experiments should be run mainly by internal teams, often mimicking what pioneers or, even worse, competitors are doing. Yet, in mature industries, companies that lack internal capabilities and knowledge might need to join forces with other players with the right skills, bold visions and conviction, or simply observe others. This is the case of Airbus and Ford, which looked outside the organization and partnered with experts—for example, NASA's Quantum Artificial Intelligence Lab—to reduce energy consumption in Ford's commercial fleets (Figure 1).

The Company is on the driving seat of the experiment	The Company coexperiments with a partner who is on the driving seat	The Company observes experiments by other players
• The Company mobilizes internal resources (ad-hoc teams) to support the design and execution of experiments • Level of Company investment and resources: medium-high • Type of experiments: answers to relevant user needs, low-risk, limited degree of complexity, plus opportunity to leverage employees as testers	• Partner conducts the experiment and the Company supports (e.g., by providing access to customer base, by contributing to specific digital tests…) in exchange of learnings (i.e. data & analyses) • Level of Company investment and resources: medium-low (main resources provided by the partner) • Type of experiments: medium-high risk, complex	• The Company monitors/studies the initiatives conducted by other players, watch others pioneering paths • Level of Company investment and resources: low (temporary intelligence teams) • Type of experiments: high-risk, very complex, limited availability of partners willing to embark on a joint experimentation

Figure 1. Criteria for selecting the right approach and building a diversified portfolio of experiments.

Enel Grids: Dispatching Field Workers with Quantum Physics

Enel Grids is Enel's global division dedicated to the management of its worldwide electricity distribution service, through 13 companies with offices in eight countries, employing more than 33,000 people directly and around 60,000 who work every day on the Group's 2.2 million kilometers of electricity networks. Enel Grids is now the largest private network operator (with more than 74 million final users) with the largest customer base (more than 70 million).

With a strong legacy of transforming distribution networks around the world into smart grids, "Enel will continue to reinforce, grow and digitize networks to enable the transition," said Enel Group's CEO Francesco Starace at the presentation of the 2023–2025 Strategic Plan. Indeed, since the launch of an ambitious digitalization program in 2016, Enel was the first large utility to become completely cloud-based. Over the years, Enel has harnessed the power of transformative technologies such as big data, machine learning (ML), and deep learning.

In 2018, on a continuous search for the next big technology, a number of Enel IT managers stumbled on an article about the future applications of quantum computing. Fascinated by the potential opportunities of this technology to unlock new ways to make Enel Grids more efficient, resilient, and sustainable, they set up a small group of tech enthusiasts, who embarked on a discovery journey. As curators, they gathered as much content as possible: they read articles, bought books, connected with leading experts and tech players—mainly early adopters—to learn more about this new technology.

As they learned along the way, they started discussing specific business problems where quantum technology could make a difference. One problem emerged as a good foundation: the traveling salesman problem. Why? Because in Enel Grids there are more than 20,000 fieldworker teams (*salesmen*) performing more than 90,000 jobs daily. Every year, Enel Grids automatically dispatches more than 32 million jobs to tens of thousands of fieldworkers and contractors in 13 distribution companies within the Enel Group.

Compared to more traditional use cases, there was no certainty about its realistic application or business effectiveness. Yet, the team knew that this quantum challenge was a complex enough problem to tackle today's high-performance computers.

Through a series of small lab experiments, the team learned how to use the various technologies and algorithms to solve the dispatching field workers problem. Some experiments were conducted internally, whereas others were performed in partnerships with experts and tech start-ups such as Data Reply. Experimentation results confirmed the quantum advantage: a 30% increase in the quality of work performed.

Four years later, the quantum-computing solution QBEAT is applied to all Enel Group's field workers in Italy (approximately 7,000 people), other potential applications are under exploration (from grid planning to investments allocation), and the small team of quantum enthusiasts has grown into a community, attracting talent from the outside the organization. They infuse quantum technology within the organization (events), monitor the latest research on quantum computing, build awareness, and nurture curiosity.

The Enel Group's experience shows that if an industry can be impacted by a new technology, waiting until it matures is not an option. It is important to gain a foothold in transformative technology to achieve a learning advantage and lay the foundations for effective future integration into the core.

Conclusion

As more and more new technologies emerge, established companies struggle to keep up with how quickly the world is transforming digitally. They wait for others to show the business value and react slowly by delegating new technological experimentation to suppliers or technological partners, without investing in developing internal knowledge and capabilities. This is a missed opportunity.

The Enel Grids example also confirms that big established companies can be smart tech pioneers in their own way. Executives with a curation mindset know that early exposure can have a long-lasting positive effect on future integration. They become more and more familiar with new technology by executing a portfolio of learning experiments and improving their ability to make better-informed decisions before new technologies become mainstream.

As traditional companies train the muscle of becoming more active and aware, the effects will be felt throughout the organization.

References

Thomke, S. (2020). *Building a culture of experimentation. Harvard Business Review*, March/April 2020. https://hbr.org/2020/03/building-a-culture-of-experimentation

https://www.enel.com/company/stories/articles/2020/12/strategic-plan-2021-2023

About the Authors

Elisa Farri is the colead of the Management Lab by Capgemini Invent and a member of the Thinkers50 Radar for 2023. By collaborating with selected faculty partners at the world's leading business schools, including Harvard Business School, MIT, IMD and LBS, the Management Lab forges new ways of thinking about strategic and organizational innovation. The Management Lab by Capgemini Invent bridges new ideas into practice, by testing and developing actionable frameworks, practices, and tools that can be applied to the real world of business. Previously, Elisa worked as associate partner at ECSI Consulting, a management research and strategic advisory center, and as researcher at Harvard Business School's Europe Research Centre in Paris. Elisa has authored several HBS case studies and is a regular contributor to leading management magazines, including HBR.org, *Dialogue Review*, the *European Business Review*, and *LSE Business Review*.

Fabio Veronese is Head of the Enel Grids Digital Hub at Enel and is responsible for the digital transformation for the Enel Distribution business. In Enel, he led the smart meter project implementation in Italy and the massive migration to the cloud of the whole IT operations of the group. Currently he is actively involved in developing an original cloud native platform approach for the development process of all the IT solutions in Enel. Fabio holds a bachelor's degree in electronic engineering from the University of Padova and a master's degree in Leadership Awareness from INSEAD.

Joint Action Model

JANKA KRINGS-KLEBE AND JÖRG SCHREINER

n today's interconnected world, people are more informed, more connected, and more demanding than ever before. This is a challenge but also an opportunity for companies, because the connectivity makes it easy to collect data about users and their behavior, to generate fine-tuned insights into their needs, and quickly offer solutions to satisfy those needs.

This highly interconnected world also changes how value is created, delivered, and captured. New technologies make room for innovations on different levels: new products, new ways of production and organization, as well as completely new ways of interaction with customers and even new markets. This shift is commonly known as digital transformation—but its implications for businesses are still largely underestimated.

To understand how fundamental this change is—and how strongly digital transformation rocks the foundations of companies—let's take a look at how they have been operating in the past.

Over decades, the most successful business models were based on ownership of mass production facilities and on gaining leadership by technological innovation. Mastering internal operations, the flow of goods, data, and money led to optimization along the entire value chain, streamlining processes and governance in favor of the main business. Being good at gradually changing and optimizing internal parts, with minimum risk to the whole and without challenging the fundamental business model—this is what companies were aiming for and it is how most of them are now trying to deal with digital transformation.

Following this logic, they approach digital transformation as another exercise in incremental change. They regard it simply as a project to modernize certain parts of the business but without touching the basic organization and its interactions. Thus, they miss leveraging the full potential of digital technology: to invent new ways of creating, delivering, and capturing value. Typical digitalization projects, therefore, are limited in their success. They succeed in modernizing some internal processes, IT, and marketing channels—and this is a good start. It lays the groundwork for the future, but it is still far away from achieving the full potential of digital transformation. The focus of such digitalization projects is solely on achieving a higher efficiency of the existing organizational setup by utilizing digital technologies. Businesses can then do more of the same. Regarding innovation, however, they are still lagging far behind technological front-runners and missing waves of new opportunities in a world that is becoming more interconnected by the hour.

In order to make meaningful progress, companies should first achieve clarity about the full extent of digital transformation and what it means for them. Digital transformation means that:

- Businesses can connect to customers in new ways;
- Value can be created, delivered, and captured in new ways;
- Work and people can be organized in new ways; and
- That all these new—and formerly unthinkable—ways are continuously changing and evolving, requiring businesses to discover new opportunities and to learn and adapt all the time.

"Many other companies believe innovation is in new products or new technologies, but we believe innovation is about developing new ways to create value for the user."

– Zhang Ruimin, chairman emeritus Haier Group (Knowledge@ Wharton, 2018)

Digital transformation, therefore, requires enabling companies to deliver on new customer expectations at a speed similar to their emergence. This in turn requires an organization that can exploit the ever-increasing market dynamic by adapting very fast—a capability that most organizations are struggling to develop. Companies have not been built with this main purpose in mind; they have been built mainly for efficiency and slow adaptation. High adaptation speeds are not possible because it would mean to let loose on efficiency or control. If both high adaptation speed and high efficiency are required, then a fundamental change of organizational and managerial principles is needed; an update is required, and in order to develop the capability for high adaptation, each company has to implement the update on its own.

The Learning Journey of Transformation

Companies need to self-discover and learn how to organize their business and internal operations in a smarter way. Developing new flexible business practices in a gradual approach has proven to be a successful path for transformation efforts. This learning journey (shown in Figure 1) is the most important step and should not be skipped; it is crucial for succeeding in the transformation and establishing corporate learning.

Figure 1. Learning journey.

As shown in Figure 1, a transformation learning journey starts small with a few teams. These teams focus on identifying what makes them slow responding or adapting to new opportunities and then trying to find ways to become faster. If they cannot solve issues on their own, then they need to report to managers with the required authority to take effective action. This typically leads to quick detection of structural or operational adaptation barriers in the whole organization.

Speed of Action

The purpose of the whole journey is on learning fast, removing emerging barriers one by one, and rapidly changing all processes and structures that are standing in the way of high adaptation speed. New-found practices need to rapidly find their way to all places in the organization where they add value. Through repetition of this process, the organization gradually develops routine and efficient managerial practices for quick and large-scale adaptation. This then institutionalized learning journey has proven to be a successful approach for transformation efforts—provided actions taken in pilot projects can quickly find their way to all relevant and affected parts of the business. Speed is of the essence: Actions need to be implemented in a timely manner, so that people see progress and can feel that their efforts make a difference. When this takes too long, people perceive it as just another bureaucratic initiative, and the organizational change grinds to a halt.

Alignment of Actions

While speed of action is priority one, priority two is the alignment of individual actions to serve overarching goals. All actions generate follow-up effects inside the organization. These effects can work against or synergistically reinforce one another. In order to have mutually supportive actions, the individual actions need to be aligned with overarching goals, communication narratives, and organizational stakeholders.

The following model of action fields provides a framework to facilitate exactly this alignment challenge (Figure 2). The model identifies six fields of action, each covering specific challenges of digital transformation and connecting them with the others. The model has proven to be a good way to start, plan, and align transformation activities of companies along their transformation journey.

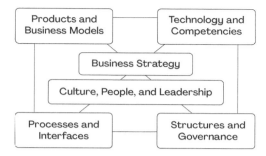

Figure 2. Action fields for digital transformation.

The action field "Products and Business Models" deals with all products and services directly delivering value to customers and generating revenue for the company.

The action field "Technology and Competencies" deals with the current and future technological capabilities and competencies required for the business.

The action field "Business Strategy" deals with the overall strategy of the company along with the processes for its deployment, execution, and adaptation.

The action field "Culture, People, and Leadership" deals with the transformation of corporate culture, leadership, peoples' attitudes, and skills.

The action field "Processes and Interfaces" deals with all processes creating value and the management of their interfaces.

The action field "Structures and Governance" deals with all organizational structures, steering processes, supporting processes, and reporting lines.

Digital transformation activities may start in one action field, but require follow-up adaptation activities in others in order to support them, remove issues caused by the activities, or create synergies. Here are some examples of how the action fields depend on one another:

- Silo-like, deeply nested organizational structures with a strong culture of bureaucracy and efficiency limit the available space for new or innovative products or business models.
- Standardized digital processes and automated interfaces can enable new business models, such as pay-per-use, that require efficient real-time tracking and charging of microtransactions. The development of such business models requires cross-domain skills in digital technology and business strategy as well as flexible structures and reporting lines.
- A business strategy of forcing business operations into markets that behave more dynamically also needs to set the conditions for these

operations to adapt quickly to their structures and processes to this market. It takes steadfast strategic leadership skills to implement such a strategy, operations with high levels of empowerment, and an entrepreneurial-minded culture.

Besides the dependencies among the action fields, they also influence one another in multiple ways:

- Roadblocks in certain fields of action can hinder progress in other fields.
- Successes in certain fields of action can enable progress in other fields.
- Each field of action is an enabler for all the others.

That is why digital transformation cannot be managed separately from other major innovation efforts, and why generating incremental improvements in single action fields won't deliver significant progress. The fields of action are interdependent and interact with one another in a complex and not exactly predictable way: New needs and dependencies of action fields emerge only during transformation. This means that transformation activities cannot be fully planned beforehand. Transparent dialogue is the only way to uncover missing parts and align activities across action fields.

Companies focusing on the principles **speed of action** and **alignment of actions** for their transformation are achieving remarkable adaptation and innovation capabilities. Amazon and Haier make high-speed adaptation capabilities a priority for their top managers. These companies are able to quickly profit from new opportunities in the market because they are never satisfied with the status quo, always willing to invest in new opportunities, and always willing to innovate their own operations. They are spawning innovation experiments every day, creating a constant flow of new ways to solve customer needs at speed and scale.

Their self-regulating, partly fractal organizational models, lead to an extreme adaptability toward market changes. Microenterprises as independent, free-standing businesses increase the resilience of Haier against market disruptions. Their ability to quickly act in concert with others allows them to react rapidly to new opportunities and fluidly scale their operations according to demand.

Ultimately, the only way for a company to stay relevant in the market is to boldly and quickly adapt to changing market conditions.

References

Krings-Klebe, J., Heinz, J., & Schreiner, J. (2017). *Future legends: Business in hyper-dynamic markets*. Tredition.

Wharton School of the University of Pennsylvania. (20 April 2018). *For Haier's Zhang Ruimin, success means creating the future.* Knowledge@Wharton. Retrieved January 12 2023. https://knowledge.wharton.upenn.edu/article/haiers-zhang-ruimin-success-means-creating-the-future/

About the Authors

Janka Krings-Klebe and **Jörg Schreiner** are founders and managing partners of co-shift GmbH, helping companies to transform into business ecosystems. They are the authors of *Future Legends: Business in Hyper-Dynamic Markets* (Tredition, 2017).

Overcoming the Resistance to Behavioral Change

KAIHAN KRIPPENDORFF

10

What holds back digital transformation the most is neither the creation of a new technology nor even the understanding of it, but rather the human adoption of it. Human adoption always lags as technology advances. Sometimes this lag can be frustratingly slow.

In 1968, for example, Dick Fosbury transformed the way that high jumpers go over high bars, turning backwards and performing what became known as the "Fosbury Flop" at the Olympics. The technology that made this possible—pads placed on the other side of high bars—had already been in place for 15 years.

Companies that engineer more rapid technology adoption can create a significant advantage. In early 2010, a few months before the Apple iPad was due to release, I was working with a large technology firm considering how they might respond to the new device. The issue was that this company already had a tablet on the market; the tablet segment was small and stagnant anyway, so they figured there was nothing else for them to do. They underestimated the importance of adoption.

Chief transformation officers and chief innovation officers can offer hundreds of similar internal examples. A new technology released for corporate use—a new training platform, marketing tool, or data analytics capability—that, once adopted, would benefit the organization but never realizes its potential because it is never adopted.

The Compounding Problem

The problems caused by the delay in human adoption of promising technologies are compounding. First, because the pace of technological advancement is accelerating as advancements shift from physical innovations (e.g., the combustion engine) to digital ones (e.g., artificial intelligence [AI]). Physical innovations generally advance in slower spurts, whereas digital innovations advance more rapidly. The engine in your car, for example, will not improve until next year's model, but the software learning how to pilot your car more effectively can improve every mile. It's hard for humans to keep up—hard for us as users, for our employees, and for our organizations to continually evolve practices as quickly as our technologies do.

Second, the problem is compounded because an inability to adapt one new technology can hinder our ability to adopt another one. For example, color TVs are a great invention but they require electricity. The color TV was first introduced in 1952. Ten years later, nearly 100% of U.S. households had one. However, even 18 years after their introduction, households in much of the world could not install a color TV because they lacked sufficient power. A fascinating study of 122 countries showed that by 1970 the energy production per capita in 56 of these countries (46%) was insufficient to power a color TV in each home.

Let's translate this dynamic into the organizational challenge of digital transformation. First, the technological advancements are less often new machines, which only come around every few years and more often digital tools, such as algorithms and AI-powered prediction machines, which improve every day. To keep up, our organizations must shift from a static to kinetic transformation mode, from transforming every few years to a state of constant evolution. If we fail to adopt one advancement quickly enough, for example, installing Internet of Things (IoT) capabilities in our products, we hinder our ability to adopt the next innovation, for example, analyzing the data provided by IoT capabilities to create more responsive machines. Each cycle of technological advancement we miss puts us at a further disadvantage. Our losses accumulate and, ultimately, we are left behind.

Customer Lifetime Value

The linchpin, then, is to enable our organizations to adopt promising technologies more rapidly than our competitors. Although this ability has always been an important driver of the longevity of an organization, digital technologies raise the stakes.

To zoom in on one specific example of a digital technology that illustrates the challenge, consider AI-enabled technologies for segmenting and predicting the value of a customer. In the past, companies could build their marketing plans on generalizations about their customer profiles. One beauty company we worked with would refer to "her" in their meetings to symbolize their core customer. When deciding what new packaging to try, product to introduce, or marketing message to use, they would debate whether a mythical "she" would prefer that packaging, product, or message. A beer company we worked with referred continually to the "beer monster" inside the thirsty customers they served.

Such generalizations are helpful implements to guide decisions but they are blunt and inaccurate. There is no exact "she" or real "beer monster"; instead, these catch-all terms help us generalize many hundreds of different types of customers, with their individual histories, preferences, and motivations.

They work because, until now, we didn't know any better. That is to say, we didn't know our customer better. We knew the average age, gender, and income of our customer but not the details of each customer. Even if we knew the specific age, gender, and income of each customer, we lacked the computing power to analyze that information. Even if we did have that computing power, we weren't able to customize our product offerings to them because they were buying predominantly physical things that we had to mass produce. Ford famously made one color of the Model T. Today's car manufacturers offer more variety but they still need to come up with makes and models that appeal to sufficiently large segments of drivers.

But things have changed. First, thanks to the proliferation of customer data, due in part to the rapid adoption of IoT, we do have enough information on the age, gender, and income of each individual customer. Additionally, we can know much more—from what they search for online to what types of food they like delivered to their homes. Second, thanks to advances in data analytics, we have the computing power to analyze this broader set of information to make more accurate predictions of what customers will like and how they will behave. Third, because more of our products' value is delivered digitally, we can customize it more accurately to the insights we derive from the expanded data we have on that customer.

These three abilities enable us to identify which customers are most valuable and to customize our offerings to them far more accurately. Companies that seize these new capabilities first will create a compounding advantage over those who are slow to do so.

Changing Behavior

We have studied the efforts of some of the world's leading companies across industries—hospitality, retail, quick-service restaurants, financial services, real estate—attempting to take advantage of the technologies that enable them to more accurately identify and serve valuable customers.

In each case, the dampening factor has been not in the understanding or installation of the technologies needed for evolution, but rather in the behavioral change needed. We spoke to numerous experts on behavioral change and looked at behavioral change models.

We found a simple, well-adopted model, called "Expectancy Theory," to be particularly helpful. The model suggests that people will adopt behavior based on the outcome they expect from that behavior. Essentially, the EPOV model can be summarized as follows:

$$E - P - O - V$$

Where E stands for "effort," P for "performance," O for "outcome," and V for "valence."

To understand this model, look at the connections between the letters rather than the letters themselves. You will put in an effort (E) if you think that will result in some performance (P). You will want to deliver on that performance if you think it will result in an outcome (O). You will want that outcome if it is something you value (V).

If any link in the chain of E to P to O to V is broken, our behavior or that of our coworkers or employees will not change, and this is illustrated as follows:

- If E to P is not linked, then we don't think we are capable. Our effort will not result in the target performance. You may want to be a professional basketball player, but you will only put in the effort (training) if you think it will result in some performance (becoming a top player on your team).
- If P to O is not linked, then you don't think your performance will result in the desired outcome. You being a top player on the team will result in the outcome of an NBA recruiter taking notice and offering you a spot on their team.
- If O to V is not linked, then you don't value the outcome your effort results in. You may think an NBA recruiter will take notice and offer you a spot on the team, but you don't value getting the spot because you don't really want to become a professional.

To activate a digital transformation, then, you need to make sure that all three links between EPOV are bridged for those employees/coworkers whose actions are required to ensure the transformation.

The Wisdom of Choosing Not to Transform

A Zen koan tells of a young monk who asks a more experienced monk what the meaning of Zen is. The experienced monk points at the moon. He says, "I could try to explain to you, but my words could only describe my finger pointing at the moon, not the moon. The problem most have with understanding Zen," he goes on to explain, "is that they confuse the finger with the moon, the words describing Zen with Zen itself."

We all fall victim to this, confusing the finger with the moon, the words with what the words are describing, the means with the ends. In the case of digital transformation, we often see organizations confusing transformation with the reason for transforming. The transformation becomes the goal itself. We forget the reason we think the company wants to transform.

The chief transformation officer, CEO, head of HR, or head of strategy starts to pursue transformation for transformation's sake. Victory looks like being able to announce to investors and the market that the company has transformed.

This is a mistake for several reasons, but most relevant here is that it tends to encourage us to pursue large-scale transformation even when a better approach is to eliminate the need for such transformation. Consider the tale of two companies implementing a technology-driven, customer-centric transformation right now. Both are large, multibillion-dollar revenue companies with operations across hundreds of markets.

The first company—let's call it Transformation Nation—realizes that its growth is about to slow down. For the past two decades, it has grown through geographical expansion, opening new markets in new territories. The issue is that the number of untapped territories is dwindling. The only way for them to maintain growth is to start convincing customers in each territory to start buying more. They decide the solution is to implement customer lifetime value (CLV), which will encourage each regional business to start increasing the value of the customers it serves by, for example, getting customers to buy more often, spend more with each transaction, and stay as loyal customers longer.

The second company—in this case we call them by their actual name, Anywhere Real Estate—is the leading residential real estate company in the United States, which also operates in certain countries outside the United States and whose brands include Coldwell Banker, Century 21, Sotheby's International Realty and Corcoran, among others.

Anywhere Real Estate realizes that one of the most important drivers of their business growth is the ability to identify real estate agents who have the greatest potential to bring in clients over the coming years.

In both cases, the company is looking to identify and attract valuable people, customers for Transformation Nation and agents for Anywhere Real Estate. These people are valuable because they will stay longer, initiate more transactions, and those transactions will be of higher value. While the goals are the same, their chosen approaches are the opposite.

Transformation Nation pursues a broad, top-down transformation. They develop a new scorecard by which to track regional performance using a new set of metrics aligned with CLV. Instead of simple revenue growth, they decide to leverage new digital capabilities that allow them to closely track customer purchases across online and offline platforms, measuring things such as purchase frequency and loyalty. This scoreboard is then cascaded down from headquarters and it is supported by many other initiatives common to broad transformation efforts such as a training program, an internal communications strategy, and encouraging regional leaders to mirror the behaviors they desire.

Anywhere Real Estate, by contrast, decides to minimize the behavioral change required. They seek to make the need for transformation irrelevant or at least diminish its necessity. Instead of a scoreboard, they develop an algorithm to help identify the most valuable agents. After much work and validation through back testing, the algorithm works. Then, instead of launching a communications and training program to convince its staff of the efficacy of this new approach, they narrow their focus. First, they identify a small set of 600 people in the company whose behaviors they want to change, in this case those people responsible for recruiting agents.

By focusing on a smaller subset of employees, they have already minimized the transformation effort. Then to further reduce it, they decide on an approach that will minimize the amount of behavioral change they ask of these people; they decide to stay within the daily workflow rather than asking people to change their workflows.

The 600 recruiters use a customer resource management (CRM) system to help manage the pipeline of external real estate agents they are attempting to recruit. Instead of trying to explain and convince recruiters of the value of their algorithm, the system puts a simple icon next to the record of any agent that the algorithm predicts will become a high performer. Rather than suggesting recruiters give different bonuses to different types of agents, the decision is simple: if the agent is marked with a specific icon, you can give them an extra signing bonus.

Now, even high-potential agents fall into ranges. Some may be superstars and others just above average. The team at Anywhere Real Estate debated creating levels of agents, distinguishing those that the algorithm predicts will become superstars from others. Although such an approach would increase the value they capture—it's worth paying higher bonuses to high-value agents—it would also increase the behavioral change and cognitive effort required of the recruiters. The team wanted to minimize the behavioral change required so they decided to stick with simplicity and classify all high-potential agents the same.

The results? While Transformation Nation is struggling to get traction, Anywhere Real Estate has crossed the finish line.

Leaders at Transformation Nation shared with us that the transformation has experienced several false starts. First, they rolled out the new scorecard and their regions seemed receptive. However, when people in a particular region sense that the head of their region is not fully bought into the new scorecard—sometimes simply because that leader asks about an old metric (revenue growth) rather than a new CLV one (repeat purchases)—they decide to default to the old scorecard. This then triggers headquarters to issue an updated scorecard in the following years, which further confuses things. Transformation Nation is not transforming.

But, then again, neither is Anywhere Real Estate. In their case, the choice is by design. Recruiters see an icon that gives them permission to offer a higher signing bonus, they offer it, they win new recruits, the algorithm (mostly) proves predictive, and those agents become more productive, ultimately resulting in more transactions, higher transaction values, and greater longevity … higher CLV.

The Lesson: Minimize the Need to Transform

Let's break down these two cases using the EPOV model (Table 1).

Table 1. Example of an EPOV Model

	Transformation Nation	**Anywhere Real Estate**
Effort	**High**: Adopt a new scorecard.	**Low to negative**: Permission given to award a higher signing bonus to those marked with a specific icon.
Performance	**Unclear**: Will following the scorecard result in higher performance for my region?	**Unchanged**: I would be recruiting these people anyway; giving them a higher signing bonus makes it easier for me to recruit them.
Outcome	**Unclear**: If our location or region performed better, would our compensation be judged by the new scorecard or the old one?	**Positive**: I receive a higher commission for signing on a high-potential agent.
Valence	**Strong**: I am motivated by my region performing well as defined by the scoreboard.	**Strong**: I am motivated by getting bonuses for signing on agents and, longer term, by my region having high-performing agents.

Conclusion

When it comes to transformation, consider whether you are interested in transformation for transformation's sake—the finger pointing at the moon, the transformation theater, training initiatives, communications, and leadership demonstrations—or transforming by reducing the effort it takes to change.

Think about the desired effect you are trying to achieve, and decide if you really need transformation to get there; it's possible that you don't. Instead, focus on minimizing the need to transform. Even if you do decide you need a broad transformation, you can minimize the effort required by taking the following steps:

- Target the number of people needed to transform (Anywhere Real Estate narrowed it down to 600 people).
- Minimize the behavior change required.

About the Author

Kaihan Krippendorff began his career with McKinsey & Company before founding growth strategy and innovation consulting firm Outthinker. Recognized by Thinkers50 as one of the top eight innovation thought leaders in the world, he is the author of five bestsellers, most recently the Edison Award nominated, *Driving Innovation from Within: A Guide for Internal Entrepreneurs*. Amid a dizzying schedule of keynote speeches, consulting projects, and ongoing research, Kaihan finds time to teach at business schools globally (including New York University and Florida International University), write regularly for *Fast Company* and other major media outlets, and play an active role on four corporate advisory boards.

Preempting Digital Disruption: The Nightmare Competitor Contest

KURT MATZLER, CHRISTIAN STADLER, AND
JULIA HAUTZ

11

Digital transformation comes in two different flavors. There is the vanilla flavor—all the great new opportunities arising from digitalization. Even before the COVID-19 pandemic forced us all to turn into digital natives, the promise of efficiency, growth, and convenience was real. A report commissioned by the UK Foreign, Commonwealth, and Development Office and other government departments found that the digital economy grew an estimated 2.5 times faster than the GDP between 2000 and 2015 (Herbert & Loudon, 2020). A more recent survey by Kearney, a consulting firm, sees this trend accelerating, noting a 300% increase in demand for online products and services (Stadler, 2021). While there is still the question of how exactly a company can benefit from digitalization, the general trajectory is positive when we focus on the new digital markets or the efficiency gains in operations.

Digital transformation, however, also comes in a licorice flavor. This much more acquired taste symbolizes the disruption that digitalization presents for many established business models. When Netflix and other streaming services first arrived on the scene, cable television providers faced a fundamental challenge to the way they were making money. Netflix subscriptions are inexpensive and there are no ad breaks during shows. Comcast and other incumbents decided to double down on the old model and increased subscription fees further and aired more ads. Not surprisingly, more customers cut the cord (Stadler et al., 2021). Netflix's new all-digital model seemed overwhelming to the old giants. Making up for the lost revenues resulting from leaving customers presented itself as an obvious way out—at least in the short term. At the same time, it accelerated the fundamental problem.

This article is about avoiding the same issue that cable companies ran into. It is about pre-empting disruption from new digital players by anticipating the threats early on and developing viable digital solutions before the insurgents come knocking on your door.

We will start by outlining the three challenges of digital disruption, followed by an introduction to war games and, finally, a step-by-step guidance through a nightmare competitor contest—an adoption of the war game logic that enables you to get ready for surprises from the digital domain.

The Three Challenges of Digital Disruption

A recent study of more than 3,600 companies in 20 industry sectors worldwide found that "68% of respondents … expect their industry to be significantly disrupted by new innovations brought by technology in the next three years" (Abbosh et al., 2018, p. 7). While companies have a variety of tools and approaches at hand to master disruptive innovation, launch corporate venture capital funds, experiment with lean start-up methodologies, cooperate with start-ups, and use open innovation (O'Reilly & Binns, 2019), digital transformation typically calls for more radical changes. It requires disruptive new business models.

A Boston Consulting Group (BCG) study found that only about one-third of companies successfully steered through disruptive changes; two-thirds went out of business, were acquired, or stumbled through years of stagnation or decline (Wick et al., 2017). Digital disruption presents companies with three distinct challenges. First, companies need to detect and correctly interpret disruptive threats. For many, this constitutes a difficult to overcome cognitive barrier. Most disruptive innovation or business models emerge from industry outsiders or newcomers (Christensen, 1997). Think Uber for taxi drivers, Airbnb for hotel groups, or Google for newspapers. Initially these offers don't even seem to be much of a threat, because existing customers do not find them appealing. But, as Andy Grove, the legendary former CEO of Intel, once said: "When spring comes, snow melts first at the periphery, because that is where it is most exposed." Hence, companies need to take an external perspective to see the early signals of disruptive change in time.

Second, seeing disruptive threats from new digital players is not enough. Companies need to commit substantial resources and prioritize disruptive digital ideas. Herein lies a significant motivational barrier. New digital entrants typically target overlooked customer segments. When Airbnb first went online, the idea to spend a night on the couch of a stranger was appealing to budget-conscious backpackers but hardly to the executives frequenting hotels. This wasn't much of a threat, or so it seemed. Incumbents, chasing higher profitability, focus on improving their existing products. They see more opportunities in preserving and defending the established business than in developing disruptions—especially when a disruptive idea cannibalizes the existing business model (Christensen & McDonald, 2015). Incumbents tend to ignore disruptive changes when their existing business is still doing fine. While profits lull them into a false sense of security, new entrants develop the disruptive business. Overcoming this *motivational barrier* of disruptive innovation is probably the biggest challenge.

After seeing the disruptive threat and committing enough resources, developing an effective response is the third challenge for incumbents. Technological convergence, in other words, "the coming together of key technologies at a particular point in time to enable the creation of an entirely new product or service at a competitive cost" (Arbib & Seba, 2020, p. 11), offers new opportunities but also new challenges. In the transportation sector, for instance, "technological and business model convergence would result in a 10x improvement in costs and capabilities of new technologies, disrupting transportation" (Arbib & Seba, 2020, p. 4) and lead to the new business model as Transportation-as-a-Service (TaaS). It's particularly difficult to find an appropriate response, considering that the digital revolution blurred industry boundaries. Monitoring competitors within your industry and adopting similar tactics is hardly a winning strategy anymore. Companies have to understand which technologies evolve outside their industries and integrate them into new and flexible business models fit for the digital world.

Tried and tested tools, such as SWOT analysis, PESTEL analysis, or Porter's Five Forces Framework won't prepare you for digital disruption. They all work on the premise of the world as it is. Strategies for the future are based on extrapolation of the past when you use these tools. When potential disruptions originate in new, alien technologies or new business models with unknown competitors from other industries, simple extrapolation is insufficient. This is a problem, not only because of the wide use of these tools, but the more general tendency of managers to rely on past information, insight, and experiences. Tensions and conflicts are the natural companions of disruption. Those loyal to the old business model will impede progress, especially when the new strategies and business models significantly depart from the current ones (Kaplan & Orlikowski, 2014). At the beginning of a disruptive process, signals of strategic threats or disruptive opportunities are weak and they are often at the periphery. Perceiving and interpreting these weak signals is difficult.

Here is the problem: "Just as the eye is designed for focus on a central area of vision with a blurry periphery, individuals and organizations are wired to see clearly what lies within their current frames and less clearly what lies in their mental shadows" (Day & Schoemaker, 2004, p. 131). It is like the difference between a flashlight and a laser beam. The laser beam has a narrow, bright, and intense focus. The flashlight provides a broad, less intense view. To detect weak signals, you need to broaden your view to see the periphery. You sacrifice intensity for scope and that's where the nightmare competitor contest comes into play. Before we explain the tool in more detail, a brief excursion into military war games helps to understand the underlying philosophy.

War Games

The Trojan Horse, Pearl Harbor, and 9/11 are three examples of surprise attacks. Neither military intelligence nor a general understanding of the enemies' intention prepared the target nations. Events like these pose a question: How can nations better handle big strategic surprises? For the past 200 years, many armies have used *war gaming* to anticipate the enemy's moves and strategies to understand the complex interactions among technologies (e.g., weapon platforms), enemies and allies, and players within the teams (Augier et al., 2018). War games are used to simulate actions and reactions. Actors use rules, data, and procedures to make decisions and these decisions lead to reactions of players representing the opposite sides (Perla, 1990).

In 1824, Georg von Reisswitz, a young lieutenant in the Prussian Army, developed one of the first war games. It consisted of a map depicting the terrain, wooden colored blocks representing the military units, and a set of rules for movement and combat. It soon became an official training tool used to test doctrines and plans. War games were so widespread and effective that the Prussian General Staff attributed the success of its army partly to the use of war games in officer training (Augier et al., 2018).

Early in the 20th century, the U.S. Naval War College became a zealous adopter of war games. In 1960, Admiral Chester Nimitz asserted: "[T]he war with Japan had been re-enacted in the game rooms here [at the Naval War College] by so many people and in so many different ways that nothing that happened during the war was a surprise—absolutely nothing except the kamikaze tactics towards the end of the war; we had not visualized those" (Hanley & John, 2017, p. 29). While this might have been an overstatement, war games allowed him to understand developments and helped adjust his strategy in the Pacific.

After World War II, during the Cold War, the war games became even more central to military planners. The RAND Corporation in particular started to adopt the approach for crisis scenarios such as a potential nuclear crisis (Hershkovitz, 2019). Today, variations of war games are played at the highest level in the U.S. Department of Defense and are practiced in a number of Fortune 500 companies (Cares & Miskel, 2007).

Research on the use of war gaming has shown two interesting effects. First, decision makers become more vigilant; they broaden the range of considered alternatives and review objectives. The Global War Games, conducted at the U.S. Naval War College before the fall of the Soviet Union, for example, led to a complete shift in thinking about strategy regarding the cooperation between U.S. naval forces and land-based forces to impede any potential Soviet aggression (Schwarz, 2011). Second, participants see early signals of change more clearly and change their mental models; in other words, their representations of assumptions, generalizations, and images of the world around them help them to simplify, create order, and reduce uncertainty.

The Nightmare Competitor Contest

To preempt digital disruption, the war game logic can be adopted in the Nightmare Competitor Contest. This exercise is distinct from war games in two important ways. First, it simulates the attack of a potential digital competitor but instead of going through a series of actions and reactions, it focuses on a single event: the emergence of a disruptive digital business model. Second, in order to take an outsider perspective, managers of an incumbent work together with select outsiders (i.e., experts in different industries, start-ups, lateral thinkers, customers, suppliers, or even potential competitors), simulating the attack of a disruptor with a new digital business model. In a two- or three-day workshop, executives, along with external experts, create hypothetical disruptors and describe their digital business models. The gamification of the process makes it easier to shake industry logic. Throughout the workshop the core question is: What could totally disrupt our current business? With that in mind, business models for digital disruptors are built. Once they are fully developed, you can use them in discussions for your own business. How can you prepare for digital disruptors of this kind? These are the steps in the nightmare competitor workshop:

Step 1. Develop a common understanding of today's business model and relevant scenarios. Scenarios are long-term trends that can pose serious threats to the business model. It is advisable that internal views are combined with external opinions to make sure that one gets a broad and complete picture of all possible scenarios.

Step 2. Set the scope. With a specific scenario in mind you can start to select participants for the workshop. A nightmare competitor workshop typically involves about 20 participants: 10 executives and internal experts and 10 external participants. It is critical that internal and external participants are equally represented. Too many internal participants, and external participants will not be heard. Too many external participants, and you will suffer from the not-invented-here-syndrome. External participants will only add value if they fit with the scope of your exercise, in other words, the broad scenarios you are interested in. Look out for relevant expertise, new perspectives and, most of all, credibility; without credibility, their opinions will not be taken seriously by the senior executives in your own company.

Step 3. Destroy your business. Participants from your own company, along with external participants, construct a potential digital disruptor who attacks your company or a particular business in your company. The use of a business model framework (e.g., our own framework composed of the five elements of positioning, product and service logic, value creation logic, marketing and sales logic, and profit formula; Matzler et al., 2013), or the business model canvas (Osterwalder & Pigneur, 2010) helps to focus the mind on those things that really matter. The participants are divided into different teams that develop the business model of the aggressor. This is done in the form of a contest—the teams compete for the best disruptive business model. The competitive spirit makes this exercise exciting and spurs creativity.

Step 4. The big vote. Ask everyone to vote for what they think is the most disruptive digital business model.

Step 5. Understand the risks and opportunities and define your strategy. This is the final phase of the nightmare competitor workshop. The implications, opportunities, and threats of the disruptive business model are detailed, and the consequences for the company elaborated, which results in a *reaction scenario*—a business model as a new digital opportunity you might pursue.

Digital transformation presents substantial growth opportunities, but for many companies breaking away from old business models this presents a substantial challenge. Worse, digital disruptors are lurking around the corner. The nightmare competitor contest helps you to figure out exactly which disruptors might be lurking, how to best preempt them, and how to become a digital disruptor yourself.

References

Abbosh, O., Moore, M., Moussavi, B., Nunes, P., & Savic, V. (2018). *Disruption need not be an enigma.* Accenture Digital Reports,.https://www. accenture. com/us-en/insight-leading-new-disruptability-index

Arbib, J., & Seba, T. (2020). *Rethinking humanity: Five foundational sector disruptions, the lifecycle of civilizations, and the coming age of freedom.* RethinkX.

Augier, M., Dew, N., Knudsen, T., & Stieglitz, N. (2018). *Organizational persistence in the use of war gaming and scenario planning. Long Range Planning, 51,* 511–525.

Cares, J., & Miskel, J. (2007). *Take your third move first. Harvard Business Review, 85,* 20–21.

Christensen, C. M. (1997). *The innovator's dilemma.* Harper Business.

Christensen, C. M., & McDonald (2015). *What is disruptive innovation? Harvard Business Review, 93,* 44–53.

Day, G. S., & Schoemaker, P. J. H. (2004). *Driving through the fog: Managing at the edge. Long Range Planning, 37,* 127–142.

Hanley, J., & John T. (2017). *Planning for the Kamikazes: Toward a theory and practice of repeated operational games. Naval War College Review, 70,* 29–48.

Herbert, G., & Loudon, L. (2020). *The size and growth potential of the digital economy in ODA-eligible countries.* K4D helpdesk report, https://opendocs.ids.ac.uk/opendocs/bitstream/handle/20.500.12413/15963/915_size_and_growth_potential_of_the_digital_economy_in_ODA-eligible_countries.pdf?sequence=1&isAllowed=y

Hershkovitz, S. (2019). *Wargame business. Naval War College Review, 72*, 67–82.

Kaplan, S., & Orlikowski, W. (2014). *Beyond forecasting: Creating new strategic narratives. MIT Sloan Management Review, 56*, 23–28.

Matzler, K., & Bailom, F., Friedrich von Den Eichen, S., & Kohler, T. (2013). *Business model innovation: Coffee triumphs for Nespresso. Journal of Business Strategy, 34*, 30–37.

O'Reilly, C., & Binns, A. J. M. (2019). *The three stages of disruptive innovation: Idea generation, incubation, and scaling. California Management Review, 61*, 49–71.

Osterwalder, A., & Pigneur, Y. (2010). *Business model generation: A handbook for visionaries, game changers, and challengers*. Wiley.

Perla, P. P. (1990). *The art of wargaming: A guide for professionals and hobbyists*. Naval Institute Press.

Schwarz, J. O. (2011). *Ex ante strategy evaluation: The case for business wargaming. Business Strategy Series, 12*, 122–135.

Stadler, C. (2021). *Catching up: 4 strategies for companies to digitalize*. Forbes https://www.forbes.com/sites/christianstadler/2021/09/09/catching-up-4-strategies-for-companies-to-digitalize/

Stadler, C., Hautz, J., Matzler, K., & Friedrich von Den Eichen, S. (2021). *Open strategy: Mastering disruption from outside the C-suite*. The MIT Press.

Wick, E., Foldesy, J., & Farley, S. (2017). *Creating value from disruption (while others disappear)*. BCG Global https://www.bcg.com/publications/2017/value-creation-strategy-transformation-creating-value-disruption-others-disappear

About the Authors

Kurt Matzler is Professor of Strategic Management at the University of Innsbruck, Austria. According to the Brightline® Initiative, he is one of the best strategic thinkers in the world. He is academic director of the Executive MBA program at MCI in Innsbruck and partner in IMP, an international consulting firm. Kurt is author of more than 300 academic papers and several books, among them he is coauthor of the German edition of *The Innovator's Dilemma* (2011), *Digital Disruption* (2016), and *Open Strategy* (MIT Press, 2021). Kurt Matzler is a passionate cyclist and a solo finisher of the Race Across America 2022.

Christian Stadler is a Professor of Strategic Management at Warwick Business School and a *Forbes* contributor. His work—most recently the award-winning book, *Open Strategy. Mastering Disruption from Outside the C-Suite*—addresses fundamental strategic questions that enable companies to grow, adapt, and consistently beat their competitors. The premier ranking of the most influential living management thinkers, Thinkers50 recognizes him as a future thinker and has shortlisted him for the Thinkers50 Strategy Award.

Julia Hautz is a Professor of Strategic Management at the University of Innsbruck, Austria, and whose work focuses on openness in organizational processes. She explores how digital technologies made corporate hierarchies and boundaries permeable to new knowledge, thereby opening up strategy making to previously excluded actors. Julia is one of the leading scholars on open strategy, substantially shaping academic debate and the emergence of a research community on this topic. In addition, she also shows that Open Strategy not only changes strategy research but fundamentally transforms the strategist's work, along with the tasks and competencies associated with the strategy profession. She is coauthor of the book *Open Strategy: Mastering Disruption from Outside the C-Suite* (The MIT Press, 2021).

Beyond Digital: Why Reimagination Is the New Execution

TERENCE MAURI

12

A series of converging and multiplying dislocations—the war in Ukraine, surging inflation, supply chain shocks, rising inequality, technological disruption, and a deep realignment of working patterns—has been an accelerant for digital transformation (e.g., remote work, automation, work from home [WFH], e-commerce, and business model evolution) and what Austrian economist Joseph Schumpeter called the "gales of creative destruction." Research by Hack Future Lab shows that, by 2025, global digital transformation spending is forecast to reach US$2.8 trillion and an estimated US$700 billion in digital transformation spending annually, which falls short of delivering the desired results. As organizations pivot from *doing* digital to *being* digital, there is a huge aspiration-to-action gap, with 67% of leaders confirming they don't have the right mindsets, culture sets, and toolsets to activate reimagination as the new execution. Hack Future Lab's research shows that most organizations miss their transformation targets, achieving less than one-third of the impact they expected from recent digital investments. Digital transformations don't fail because of technology—they fail because of sociology and psychology. A mandate for reimagination as the new execution has never been more urgent.

New contexts demand new questions. Leaders get to take advantage of the questions they ask and turn turbulence into a platform for bold transformation, learning, and experimentation. Questions are like a golden key that can unlock the door to new ways of thinking and seeing the world and is a catalyst for reimagination.

Which of the following are the boldest questions you will ask today?

- What are the mindset shifts, blind spots, and frameworks for reimagination as the new execution?
- What can leaders learn from the best performers about how to beat the odds of transformations failing?
- Are you learning and unlearning at the speed of the customer?
- Which bold moves and biggest reframing moments will you leverage to start writing your organization's future success headlines today?

A Change in Perspective is Worth at Least 80 IQ Points

The big story for 2023: Leaders should not waste one of the biggest reframing moments of their lifetimes! It's not just about technology and trends—it's about choices and consequences too, whether that be recession risk, inflation risk, or rate risk. Everything the internet did to music and newspapers is now happening to everyone else. We're living in a world of venture-backed unicorns and decacorns that are scaling up and transforming markets as varied as fintech, electric vehicles, and healthcare.

This is the new meta and has nothing to do with Facebook. It means competitive lines redrawn, entire industries upended, capital markets and business strategies reshaped, and the nature of value creation redefined. Whether it's the platformization of consumer financial services or the rise of the metaverse, cost advantages and barriers to entry based on physical assets break apart; new business models, new market entrants, and new winners emerge. Given this, it is worth remembering that leaders always have blind spots and so, too, do organizations. Every organization needs to pay attention to the *baseline fallacy*, which is the assumption that the current successful business model is a low-risk bet until it isn't, at which time it is too late to do anything about it. Leaders now drop from hero to zero faster and the half-life of competitive advantage is one year and less (e.g., Netflix shares fell over 70% in 2022, wiping billions off its market cap and becoming one of the worst-performing stocks in the S&P 500). This means that long-term, sustained success becomes harder and rarer, and leaders become prisoners of the mental models of their past and current successes. Success corrupts success, and failures to imagine new businesses are really failures of reimagination.

You Can't Explore a New World With an Old Map

Every organization starts as an act of imagination but to sustain vitality for the long-term requires reimagination, which I define as the human force that pushes you to persist in the face of inertia and difficulty and see your transformation through to a successful conclusion. Reimagination—adapting a core business to disruptive change while also creating new growth around new products, business models, platforms, or ecosystems—may be the leadership imperative of the 21st century. It's the curiosity to learn and the courage to unlearn. Learning helps you transform and unlearning helps you stay ahead of disruption as witnessed by reimagination pioneers, such as Tata, Microsoft, DBS, Hermés, Ocado, and Estée Lauder, for building meaningful new digital business models despite their complex legacy businesses. Reimagination starts with digital obsession, high learning orientation, an aligned view of the future, and an enterprise-wide set of bold imperatives (e.g., strengthen identity, agility, and scalability) that reframe the world around you in radically new ways, turning uncertainty into a tailwind for light speed transformation and accelerated growth. The disruptive trends that threaten to indelibly reshape every vertical over the next five years—disintermediation in the supply chains, erosion of traditional economies of scale advantages, and more companies dying younger—will only accelerate. The question is: As leaders, how do you capitalize on the disruptive forces of the last few years and shape the future with intentionality?

Embrace the New Logic of Competition

Today, five innovation platforms (blockchain, energy storage, artificial intelligence [AI], robotics, and DNA sequencing) are converging in ways that will create huge shifts in the logic of competition and the future of leadership. Hack Future Lab's research shows that in the last two years, companies associated with these five innovation platforms have doubled their equity market capitalizations from US$7 trillion to US$14 trillion. The next 10 years will continue to scale exponentially, creating tremendous risk but also tremendous opportunity. Risk and reward travel together. Your next competitor could come from a completely different industry, leveraging hyperautomation, decentralized governance, and cloud technologies with 90% lower operating costs. To put that into perspective, digital giant Shein is now worth the same as Elon Musk's SpaceX as well as H&M and Zara, if these two *were combined. This is the new logic of competition: wide versus narrow digital moats, network effects, speed of scale, speed of innovation, talent density, visionary capital, and algorithms that learn at the speed of the customer.* It's no longer organizations versus organizations; it's mindsets versus mindsets and cultures versus cultures. You're now competing on:

- Rate of learning and high-risk tolerance for failure and anomalies, which are sources of innovation. As the ratio of assumptions to knowledge increases, so must the rates of experimenting and exploring.
- Ecosystems built from communities, relationships, and networks.
- Culture as an accelerant and a way of attracting and retaining talent; the number one reason why talent follows money is a lack of internal growth and mobility.
- In trust we grow (trust is the currency of transformations, and yet 10 out of 15 organizations have operated at the edge of ethics in the last five years, e.g., data privacy breaches, tainted foods and, tragically, even loss of life).
- Speed of decision-making; for example, only 20% of leaders excel at decision-making and only 41% can link decisions to enterprise value and strategy.
- Automation, augmentation, and digitization where, according to Microsoft, IT spending will jump from 5% to 10% of GDP in the next five years, and the remaining 80% of organizations will re-platform to the cloud.
- ROI—not just return on investment but new human metrics for a new world: return on intelligence and return on imagination (every business is an act of imagination).

I don't believe that turbulence itself is the biggest threat to an organization's existence. I believe the biggest threat is acting with yesterday's thinking, assumptions, and mental maps that are no longer relevant. Embracing the new logic of competition requires leaders to step up—simultaneously performing while transforming, leading vertically and horizontally, influencing beyond the organization, and impacting ecosystems of trust excellence.

Lead From the Future

The future favors the bold. Leaders are currently stuck between the certainties of the past and the unknowns of the future. Leaders that harness reimagination include Moderna, for reimagining pharma using mRNA—the software of life; Beyond Meat, for reimagining food technology for a healthy and ecologically friendly future; and Klarna, the buy now, pay later decacorn disrupting the US$8 trillion credit card payment market.

Organizations that decide to lead from the future, not the past, exhibit several universal behaviors in their reimagination journey, which I call DELTAs—distinct elements of transformation:

1. **Wide-spread agility:** Pivot to workforce ecosystems and AI-powered talent marketplaces (e.g., Gloat, Inc.).

2. **Optimized reality:** When everyone digitalizes, going deep differentiates (e.g., vertical integration).

3. **War for talent:** Move from talent hoarding to talent creation and enablement (e.g., map skills taxonomy) and go deep on talent density.

4. **Learning:** Explore early to exploit know-how and learn and experiment sooner (e.g., return on intelligence).

5. **Culture:** Scale cultures of curiosity over cultures of conformity.

6. **Human-centric leadership:** Use care and cocreation leadership styles over command and control.

7. **Data:** Empower teams by democratizing data and codesign the transformation journey (e.g., Airbnb's Data University program).

8. **Inclusivity at scale:** Go big on believing (meaning), belonging (community), and becoming (personal growth).

9. **Reduce bureaucratic mass index** (e.g., run a radical simplification month).

10. **Unlearn:** As the rate of transformation accelerates, the rate of unlearning must match it.

One of the biggest leadership paradoxes of our time is that technology changes fast but humans don't. Leaders are trapped in a wisdom gap with the complexities of runaway technology outstripping our human brains' capacity to make sense of it all (e.g., consider that the processing power of a computer chip has increased over one trillion times). Additionally, although technology isn't the only reason, runaway technology is rapidly widening the gap even further, leading to organizational or structural stupidity. For example, the number of words in the U.S. tax code has increased from 400,000 to four million in the last 20 years, highlighting a human bias toward bureaucratic bloat and adding complexity to complexity. To lead from the future, leaders reject *present forward* ways of thinking that simply extend existing assumptions and operating models to the future. Instead, leaders should emphasize culture setting, direction setting, and pacesetting. Biopharmaceutical leader Pfizer champions this principle by saying that transformations fail because organizations fail to transform their people. To be reinvention ready, it cultivates cultures of care and curiosity that welcome ideas that challenge the status quo versus cultures of control and conformity that reject ideas that challenge the status quo.

Attention is the New Oil

Data isn't the new oil. Attention is the new oil: attention to macro trends shaping the future, attention to adopting new agile ways of working and saying goodbye to the status quo, and attention to sustainable growth and responsible capitalism. A leader's attention is under constant attack when it comes to navigating the future and sustaining long-term vitality. Research at Hack Future Lab shows that attention—and leadership attention in particular—has exploded into millions of fragmented pixels, and the accelerants have been digitization, automation, and social media. This research shows that:

- Ninety-three percent of leaders believe their leadership attention is key to digital transformation but only 27% believe it's a strength.
- Sixty-eight percent of leaders report either themselves or their teams are at risk of digital overload and overwhelm.
- Sixty-five percent of the business decisions made today are more complex than those made two years ago.
- Forty-nine percent of leaders believe their digital transformation strategy is fragmented.

The number one takeaway is that leaders embarking on the reimagination journey are tired. Zoom fatigue. Meeting fatigue. Collaboration fatigue. Complexity fatigue. Transformation fatigue. A key takeaway is that you can't achieve sustainable transformation without deep leadership and a bold reimagination narrative about what stays, what changes, and what goes. With 93% of leaders expecting significant technological disruption over the next three years, leaders say they must adapt their mindset and pace to the new context or lose relevance.

Leaders have selected these initiatives as their top three priorities:

27% of leaders: agility

25% of leaders: driving culture and transformation

13% of leaders: mapping talent to value

13% of leaders: putting purpose to work

9% of leaders: simplifying the organization

5% of leaders: virtualizing work

8% of leaders: other

To avoid strategy, transformation, or culture drift, leaders and their teams must choose a path of meta-attention to three imperatives:

Who we are (identity): Sharpen the purpose and trust agenda.

How we decide (agility): Activate widespread agility and speed of decision-making.

How we grow (scalability): Promote inclusive and sustainable growth; rethink capability stacks around data and value creation.

We've moved from a complicated world (linear, predictable, and rules-based) to a complex world (non-linear, unpredictable, and fluid) and this demands leaders. Leaders must deal with the complex demands of leading for today while reimagining for tomorrow. Leaders pay a high leadership tax every time their attention is diverted by a pointless meeting or another back-to-back Zoom call. Here is what you can do differently today to help your organization sustain the highest return on attention, which is the key to leading a human-led, tech-enabled transformation:

1. **Focus on velocity, not speed.**
   The reason is simple. Speed is the time rate at which you're moving along a path, whereas velocity is the rate and direction. Speed without aligned direction can impede transformation initiatives and waste precious talent, motivation, and leadership resources.

2. **Fight complexity with simplicity.**
   When you run into a problem you can't solve, don't make it smaller— make it bigger. Today's transformation challenges can't be solved with yesterday's thinking. Transformation is no longer a program. It's not linear. Thinking small and adopting an incrementalist perspective depletes the ambition and energy needed to make things happen. Take coresponsibility for reimagination and embrace the urgency and scale of your biggest transformation challenges.

3. **The surprising truth of no meetings.**
   It sounds obvious, but you're having too many meetings. Hack Future Lab's research highlights that the number of back-to-back meetings

has doubled and are often scheduled with no breaks in between. Too many wasteful meetings lead to a higher cognitive and leadership tax. Having a meeting-free day increases autonomy, engagement, focus, and commitment to transformation by 5.8 times.

4. **Have a no strategy.**
   Hack Future Lab's research highlights that 83% of leaders are drowning in too many priorities and overcommitments. This erodes leadership attention and is a significant transformation derailer. A no strategy is one of the best forms of optimization and a proven way to protect collective commitment to the transformation journey. It's your workforce and transformation multiplier.

Reimagination is Your North Star

Transformation failure can be defined as an organization's inability to unlearn the always done ways, turn uncertainty into action, and unlock the imagination of their employers' even when doing so will sustain vitality, renew their lease on the future, and capture more value creation. Leaders always overestimate the risk of trying something new and underestimate the risk of standing still. When uncertainty is high, not taking a risk is a risk. So, what can you do differently today to start the journey of reimagination as the new execution? Without reimagination, leadership breaks down, organizations die younger, people stop learning, and cultures decay. In an age with record levels of social tension, economic nationalism, and technological revolution, it's time for leaders to put reimagination at the forefront of their purpose, strategy, and transformation goals and use it as their North Star for navigating deep uncertainty and complex futures. The Japanese word Henka (変化) means perpetual change, courage, and transcendence and takes its inspiration from nature. It's turning lead into gold, oil into water, or a caterpillar into a butterfly. It's the quintessence of reimagination. When the future arrives faster than ever before, will you watch the world change around you and cling to the past or be the one leading it with reimagination as the new execution?

About the Author

Terence Mauri has been described as "an influential and outspoken thinker on the future of leadership" by Thinkers50. He is the founder of a global management think tank, Hack Future Lab, entrepreneur mentor at MIT, and an adjunct professor at IE Business School, where he lectures on the Advanced Management Program. His most recent book is *The 3D Leader: Take Your Leadership to the Next Dimension* (FT Publishing, 2020).

Citizen Development: Bridging the Gap Between the Business and IT

DALIBOR NINKOVIC AND LAURA FAUGHTENBERRY

nnovating and growing your business in today's everchanging, competitive world is crucial to turning ideas into viable software solutions. Creating new and innovative value through digital solutions is the foundation of any digital transformation initiative within an organization. Yet, IT departments are overwhelmed by demand coming from the business. As demand increases, so does IT backlog; as a result, organizations are falling behind on their digital transformation projects. This hinderance is underpinned by the lack of professional IT developers and the fact that some organizations are still using traditional software development technologies to write code from scratch. The extra strike for businesses is a misalignment between the business and the IT department. Some organizations have worked to create better alignment between departments over the years, but this is more the exception than the rule.

In this article, we'll look at citizen development and how it can help to bridge the gap between the business and the IT department. Before we dive deeper, let's clarify the terms "citizen development" and "citizen developer".

Citizen development describes the ability for a user—the citizen developer—to create applications without coding expertise, significantly faster, and at a fraction of the cost. Gartner's original definition of the term citizen developer is:

> "A citizen developer is an employee who creates application capabilities for consumption by themselves or others, using tools that are not actively forbidden by IT or business units. A citizen developer is a persona, not a title or targeted role. They report to a business unit or function other than IT.
>
> All citizen developers are business technologists. However, all business technologists are not necessarily citizen developers. There is no required designation of proficiency or time allocation for citizen developers, but they must be legal employees of an organization (Gartner)."

As we can see, we are now entering the realms of business professionals creating software applications. Is this a good or bad idea? Let's refer to Figure 1 to define the environment and discuss it.

Figure 1. The evolution of technology and the emergence of citizen development.

Traditionally, software developers have always written code, but methodologies have changed over time.

First, there is the waterfall approach, where businesses can write the requirements and submit these to the development team for delivery. One of the major issues with this approach, in addition to being slow, is that there is no scope for change. The business waits for the final delivery, which may or may not be what they asked for; therefore, misalignment is almost inevitable.

Then, there's the agile approach, created to address misalignment issues through a reiterative approach to better meet requirements; however, code is still required to be written, and delivery times often don't meet the demands of the business.

Enter low-code and no-code platforms (LCNC). The emergence of these platforms came at a time when there was a demand to deliver software solutions more efficiently, and the need for software developers was on the rise. The number of trained developers was not meeting the need. These platforms allow users—through the use of drag and drop and/or point and click functionality—to create software applications and automate workflows with little to no coding skills. They empower a completely new breed of developers: citizen developers.

The requirements are no longer written in most of the cases but, rather, through a hyperagile approach, realized immediately in the form of a prototype or even a minimum viable product (MVP). This is possible by having business professionals themselves convert their requirements into a software application, which is then either rolled out into production or passed over to the IT department for a finished product. The complexity of the applications that are being built will determine if this approach is possible and will be decided on a per project basis but what this approach does do well is bridging the gap between the business and IT in terms of what is actually required from the application. Business domain knowledge holders are now realizing their requirements and turning ideas into software applications directly instead of writing the requirements in a document.

Business departments have always been doing things outside of the IT governance scope. Whether in the forms of complex VBA (Visual Basic Analysis) scripts, thousands of MS Excel spreadsheets and MS Access databases, or even deploying bespoke and/or off-the-shelf systems to solve their immediate department challenges. This term is generally known as a "shadow IT" and describes the use of IT systems, applications, devices, and similar tools without explicit approval from the IT department. The reason many business users opted for shadow IT was to work more efficiently and drive innovation. They might have felt like it took too long for IT departments to deliver their solutions due to growing requirements or they felt it was nearly impossible to convert their business requirements into something IT could deliver. Unfortunately, shadow IT also introduced serious security risks through data leaks, compliance violations, and maintenance issues.

Innovation—the ultimate goal of any digital transformation project—comes from the business users but it can only be realized in an IT sanctioned and governed environment. This is the founding principle of any citizen development initiative.

Many organizations have successfully embraced citizen development. These organizations have achieved unprecedented levels of innovation, business efficiency, cost saving, and employee and customer satisfaction, whereas others have failed with their citizen development initiatives. One of the main reasons for these failures is that these companies started by embracing the new LCNC technology inside business departments without fully understanding the risks and still trying to work without the IT department's involvement and without standards and training, projects turned into shadow IT.

Project Management Institute (PMI) and FTI Consulting surveyed over 1,600 people to ascertain the need for citizen development in the market. Results showed 79% of IT leaders agree that it is critical to have an independent organization set the standards for citizen development. In addition, 9 out of 10 of these IT leaders agree that to give more autonomy to business users, it is important to provide training. The results also showed that LCNC tools would be used over 70% more if training was provided. PMI developed a citizen development framework called the "Citizen Development Canvas" (Figure 2).

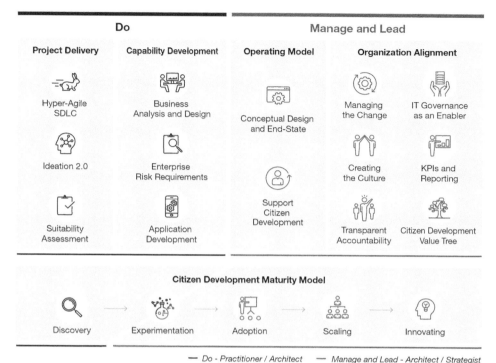

Figure 2. The Citizen Development Canvas.

The Citizen Development Canvas brings clarity and guidance to the methods by which citizen development should occur; defines the structures and competencies required to make it happen effectively; and establishes the approach necessary to introduce, scale, and manage citizen development within an enterprise.

This framework describes the five major components that allow an organization to successfully build, operate, and scale apps across an organization.

The first two areas on the canvas fall under the heading of "Do." These are the Project Delivery and Capability Development steps. Project Delivery caters to the nuances of citizen development, providing accessible tools that help with the development of applications in the appropriate way. Capability Development provides the tools required to design and develop applications within the context of the wider business.

The second two areas, Operating Model and Organizational Alignment, fall under the Manage and Lead heading. These deal with the management and operational issues involved in an organization's adoption of citizen development. These involve both the citizen developer business architect and citizen developer strategist and each plays important roles. In most cases, the strategist chooses the model and approach, while the business architect executes, manages, and oversees the process.

At the bottom of the canvas, there is a five-stage Maturity Model that allows organizations to assess, diagnose, and remedy obstacles or identify actions to help them pursue an effective citizen development strategy. A concerted citizen development strategy at scale requires unique structures, tools, processes, and practices embedded in the organization to enable value delivery through citizen development.

The Maturity Model stages are Discovery, Experimentation, Adoption, Scaling, and Innovating.

The Citizen Development Canvas offers organizations a comprehensive methodology and framework to successfully integrate citizen development into their ways of working. It is the only vendor-agnostic framework currently available.

Innovation-driven digital transformation projects are more likely to have higher rates of success when utilizing citizen development in a governed and risk mitigated way. There are so many technology options available on the market that nonprofessional software developers can use to create applications. If we unlock business domain knowledge that is seemingly locked inside the business departments to create new, innovative solutions, then we have the potential to reduce IT backlogs.

Some IT departments are still a bit resistant to the idea of citizen development because they worry it is just another version of shadow IT; however, when citizen development is governed, this is not the case. Citizen development does not mean business users use LCNC platforms without IT playing a major role in the process. IT must be part of these initiatives. The chosen LCNC platform(s) must be sanctioned by IT to ensure "the correct fit"; however, the right balance of governance must be struck. Too much governance will discourage business users and prevent the innovation.

In addition, not every project is suitable for citizen development. Some projects can be fast tracked and fully developed and delivered by citizen developers. Some need assistance from IT and other, more complex, projects should not even be attempted by citizen developers and should be fully owned by IT departments. PMI's framework provides you with tools to determine a project's citizen development suitability (Figure 3).

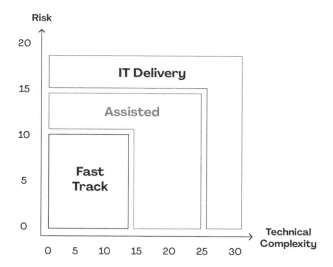

Figure 3. Software Development Life Cycle (SDLC) path based on risk and technical complexity.

In essence, IT departments should not fear citizen development but embrace it instead. Citizen development allows IT departments to focus on crucial, core systems projects and reduce their backlog by removing small projects from their workload.

When starting a citizen development initiative inside an organization, it is imperative to establish a core group. This group should sit outside the IT department but include IT team members. Some organizations call this group a center of excellence (CoE), others create their own names this group. The key is to have a group that represents everyone with an interest in the value delivery promised by citizen development.

As with any major initiative, there needs to be centralized accountability for a citizen development program in which all activities will be monitored and managed. This group will own the governance strategy and be responsible for monitoring and ensuring that all citizen development activities follow the rules. This entity will direct the citizen development program completely and will also:

- Implement and maintain citizen development policies and guidelines;
- Provide resources;
- Organize activities, trainings, and facilitate a community for citizen developers;
- Assume responsibility for managing the platforms and systems that citizen developers use to build;

- Catalog, maintain, and publish a list of relevant data services and APIs (Application Programming Interfaces); and
- Report on the status of the program to internal and external stakeholders.

The key to success is to have a multidisciplinary team in close collaboration with the IT department. Organizations where the IT department assumes responsibility for the sanctioned use of a platform on which citizen developers can work, will stand a greater chance of making the citizen development initiative work.

This is how citizen development will bridge that gap between the business and IT.

There is one aspect of citizen development we haven't talked about yet but it is equally important for success: the growth mindset required for the successful citizen development program and the cultural impact of such a program.

The role of a project manager is evolving. The project manager interacts with various departments across the business and often can be the best person to identify where gaps exist. Being able to point to instances where manual processes could be automated or when something is inefficient and not ideal can help improve employee and customer experiences. Citizen development training can play a huge role in advancing a company's digital transformation by enabling employees to understand how they can do more with less.

The success of a citizen development program inside the organization is not theoretical and supported by many organizations, which have embraced citizen development programs as part of their digital transformation projects. For example, Amtrak formally adopted a citizen development program in 2020 with six people participating and a total of 16 applications. As of 1 January 2023, Amtrak's CitDev program has reached 478 developers with 4,985 applications, touching every business area in the company. The result of this program is a savings of US$76 million and over 1.2 million personnel hours returned to the company.

In another example, Shell decided to empower its workforce through citizen development (Bratincevic, 2022). As their adoption of low-code, no-code software development technologies scales up fast, a search of the marketplace led them to the PMI Citizen Developer™ suite of resources to help them deliver training on industry standards, best practices, and governance.

From the get-go Shell set out to train 500 DIY developers and have trained more than 6,500, with participation from many business areas and roles.

More than 4,000 of those trained are actively developing. They now have 170 DIY coaches, mostly volunteers, with 44% of coaches coming from non-IT roles in their business areas.

In conclusion, citizen development is an accelerator for any digital transformation project. The organizational benefits span many areas: accelerated innovation, increased competitiveness, cost savings/revenue increase to exponentially increased customer services, and employee satisfaction. Business departments benefit from increased job satisfaction and productivity along with better collaboration with IT. IT departments will remain in control, but they benefit by the decrease in backlogs as well as an increase in job satisfaction through clear focus on the core rather than on trivial tasks.

Citizen development is the only way to bridge the ever-widening gap between business and IT.

References

Bratincevic, J. (2022). *How Shell led a citizen developer movement.* Forrester.. https://www.forrester.com/blogs/how-shell-led-a-citizen-developer-movement/

Gartner. https://www.gartner.com/en/information-technology/glossary/citizen-developer

Project Management Institute (PMI). PMI Citizen Developer™. https://www.pmi.org/citizen-developer

About the Authors

Dalibor (Dali) Ninkovic is responsible for PMI Citizen Developer™ global B2C and Community business. Over the years, Dali has worked in the low-code and no-code industry through a variety of both, technical as well as commercial roles before joining PMI and firmly believes in democratization of software development.

Laura Faughtenberry was the Product Marketing Lead for PMI Citizen Developer™. She's an award-winning marketer who's worked in the training industry and for various SaaS companies. Laura enjoys positioning solutions and finding creative ways to tell stories. Prior to becoming a marketer, she was a TV journalist.

The Five Questions to Answer in Your Digitalization Strategy

JOSEF OEHMEN AND UDO HIELSCHER

O ver recent years, the DTU (Technical University of Denmark) RiskLab has worked with many large organizations on a seemingly simple question: How can we implement artificial intelligence (AI) capabilities into our core business processes? In our case, the focus was on project risk management. The organizations are responsible for very large CAPEX projects, and deficiencies in project risk management were frequently quoted as one of the main root causes underlying cost overruns and schedule delays. So, it seemed like an obvious choice to make investments into the most advanced tools at our disposal to improve our organization's risk management performance. Since everyone is talking about AI, how hard can it be? The short answer is this: You can do it, but it requires careful work. From a strategic and governance perspective, the most critical contribution is to ask the right questions, set the right challenges for your team, and appreciate the critical paradoxes that are holding back many organizations from a more aggressive adoption of advanced digital tools. This article will illuminate five core paradoxes and the associated questions your teams need to overcome. We believe that many of the questions we encountered are also relevant for the implementation of less buzzword-like digitalization initiatives outside of AI and machine learning (ML) such as robotic process automation (RPA) or implementations of core operational new enterprise resource planning (ERP) or customer relationship management (CRM) systems.

A previous book in this series, *The Chief Strategy Officer Playbook*, discussed how discovery, experimentation, scaling, and operational excellence are the four core activities when leading digital transformations in organizations. The following discussion provides useful guidance for both discovery and experimentation activities and outlines fundamental questions associated with them.

Question 1: What business problem are we solving?

The first important question to ask in your conversations defining your digitalization strategy is based on a paradox the DTU RiskLab observed many times in the studied organizations: on the one hand, everyone in the room was excited about—and sometimes absolutely convinced—that advanced AI and ML capabilities are the new frontier of competitive advantage. AI leadership is the new must-win battle for running a cost-effective and capable organization and key to managing today's and tomorrow's complexity. However, when asked about concrete use cases (or examples), where these new capabilities would generate tangible business benefits today, the discussions quickly became bogged down in speculations of varying degrees of creativity. We may argue that it is appropriate—and it is to a certain degree—as we are discussing cutting-edge technologies that are new to us. However, arguing for a first-of-a-kind demonstrator project using advanced AI capabilities in, for example, project risk identification, is a very different proposition than adopting an RPA system as customer number 1,500 of that vendor.

In both cases, the first important question is the same: what hands-on business problem are we solving by implementing either a demonstrated or hypothesized advanced-digital capability? Even if we are pursuing a first-of-a-kind experimentation in our industry, we should be very clear about the specific processes we are targeting; how our new AI tool will change its result; what the specific AI contribution is; and how it will integrate with the current process (and humans). The fact that our understanding of specific business impact will evolve (and should), as we run our first experiments and demonstrators, is no excuse for embarking on an ambitious digitalization journey without a very clearly articulated problem that is being solved or concrete benefit that is provided above the status quo. Specifically, we typically ask three questions: First, which key stakeholders are affected by the digitalization? There are two large groups. The first group are the people affected operationally, in other words, the people involved in executing the current process and the future digital process, including those affected by new or changed requirements for data availability (in terms of quality, granularity, and timeliness). The second group is equally important and made up of the internal and/or external customers, or users, of the analytical insights or automations being implemented. What are their expectations of being able to use the results in their workflows, both in terms of content and presentation? Second, what is the formal, official problem that is being solved? Is it increased accuracy of forecasts? If yes, why, and how will that benefit us? Is it the identification of certain trends? If yes, how will that help us relative to our current practice, and how will we make decisions based on the new insights? And, third, what is the *real* (or unofficial) problem? What are the internal political and cultural contexts? Is this happening as a reaction to an economic recession or is this, for example, part of a growth and innovation portfolio (where arguably there is more support, if maybe a lack of capability to develop and implement solutions)?

Question 2: What data will we use?

There is another fun paradox underlying this question: On the one hand, many organizations we have worked with have started to eagerly collect and sometimes structure data, which is done with some enthusiasm as there is general opinion that data is the raw material of the future so the more we have, the better. Arbitrarily collecting data often is also not particularly expensive or difficult, thus a relatively easy way of showing progress toward a digitalization agenda. On the other hand, organizations spend relatively little time actually maintaining (including the removal of obsolete data) and using the data. I would risk a bet that sharing data used versus data collected has become smaller over recent years—data collection is currently outgrowing data use. For example, in one organization the entire management team was eager to implement a more data-driven, decision-making framework. Everyone agreed that the current quality of data was not sufficient to support it. However, the CIO still failed to argue for increased investments into data management. Why? Because investments of such a nature rightfully ask for a convincing business case. The existing data quality was so poor, however, that it was hard to explore possible practical applications (and their associated business benefits). The organization was stuck in a situation where a foundational investment in data quality was impossible to justify, because the data quality was so poor.

We typically ask three questions regarding data use. First, and most importantly, what data do we have that is actually usable for data analytics? This requires us to involve a data analytics expert working with the available data to provide an assessment. A simple statement of "we have a decade of historical data" may be a goldmine—it may just as likely (probably more likely) take at least 6 to 12 months of hard work to define a basic data architecture and ingestion mechanism before we can even start to form an opinion on data quality. The second question takes a different perspective, not from the data side, but from the algorithm side, so to speak: What data do we need and who has access to that data? Here, we imagine a world where data is available at the push of a button: What specifically would we need, how quickly, and how often? Who would be responsible for collecting and coding it? How would we ensure and monitor quality? This again requires a mature understanding of the type of analytics that we expect to execute. And, finally, the third and maybe most important question: How much money are we willing to spend on data? Organizations often work under the assumption that data is free. We use computers to run our processes, so how hard can it be to collect data? The reality is that usable data may eventually be cheap to collect, but initially creating processes and systems that allow us to harvest data are not free, especially if what we are interested in is not easily captured in numbers (e.g., customers trust in our brand). This includes activities to define data needs and data architectures that enable their exploration and use.

Question 3: What analytical capability do we actually need?

We think that having many choices is a good thing. Think of my kids walking into a candy store with wall-to-wall shelves of hundreds of types of candy. Their eyes light up, they run in, try to touch everything, giggle. Then, after a while, they start staring blankly at the walls of sugary promises. Eventually, we walk out with the same three kinds of candy we would have bought in the corner store. Truth is, many organizations are a little like kids when it comes to digitalization. There is so much choice, so much promise, and it is so difficult to make a decision when we have hundreds of options before us. This presents us with a very difficult challenge when exploring priority areas for advancing the digital agenda. The most important takeaway from our work is that we cannot outsource the discovery work of identifying technology trends that are useful to our organization. We cannot rely on consultants or academics to appreciate our needs. One option is to decide firmly to be a second or third mover and wait for other players in our industry to do the discovery and experimentation work for us. Another option is to invest in technology scouting and roadmapping and embrace the complexity that comes with advanced analytics.

To start, we typically break down advanced analytical capabilities into five categories:

1. **Descriptive capabilities:** Our ability to collect and visualize lightly processed (cleaned up) raw data, which helps us understand a current status quo or a snapshot of a point in time in the past. Examples include project management or production dashboards that create transparency regarding current performance levels. Anyone who ever got a dashboard to work and used it in decision-making knows this is already a tall order in many organizations. A simple example of this is: "Our data shows that we had 10 mm of rainfall in the last 24 hours."

2. **Diagnostic capabilities:** These add evaluations and judgments to the data we see. These capabilities often rely on understanding trends and time series and being able to discern good trends from bad trends. This also applies to the interpretation of single values and observations, helping decision makers to focus their attention on critical areas that require immediate attention. In our weather example: "10 mm of rainfall in the last 24 hours is no cause for concern."

3. **Predictive capabilities:** The focus of the analytical capabilities now starts focusing on predicting future developments by extrapolating or otherwise modeling existing data. This not only requires that sufficient amounts of relevant data are available to execute predictive models but it also requires the development, training, and testing of those models. A critical challenge here is the specificity of the models being used—if they are too generic, they provide limited accuracy to the specific use case; if they are too specific, on the other hand, it is often impossible to gather enough data (and commit the resources) for the training and testing. Again, in our weather example: "It rained 10 mm in the last 24 hours, but there is plausible concern for 150 mm of rainfall in the next 24 hours."

4. **Prescriptive capabilities:** The question now shifts from "What will happen in the future?" to "What action should we take and when?" This links data and its interpretation with models that describe possible actions and their consequences. These can take simple forms of triggering specific reserved actions when well-defined quantitative indicators are exceeded. More complex forms are iterative optimization models where a larger number of decisions over longer time frames are explored and options for ideal or robust decision-making pathways are developed and presented to decision makers. In our weather example, a prescriptive model may raise an alarm and suggest not traveling and taking action to secure facilities against flooding.

5. **Cognitive capabilities:** In the final category, we summarize capabilities of algorithms to execute pattern recognition tasks and discover associations within the data not already explicitly modeled. This can include, for example, exploring unstructured data sets for bottom-up pattern recognition, causal associations among events in time-series data, categorization of events and their consequences, identification of network effects, or semantic interpretation and analysis of natural language type data. Although this category of capabilities may most often be intuitively associated with the idea of artificial intelligence, organizations require significant experience in data analytics and the associated practicalities of data management and modeling to start exploring these capabilities. In our weather example, a model may alert us that strong rainfall is also associated with strong winds and power outages, and that additional actions are required to mitigate the most significant risks.

Future AI Use in Project Management at Bosch

Diagnostic Capabilities: Dashboard to Visualize and Explore Project, Program, and Portfolio Risk Profiles

Dashboards integrate numerous project risk management tools, providing a cross-business unit risk analysis on a large number of programs with drill-down ability into single projects. Technology wise, these dashboards have become much easier to implement once the risk data from a diverse range of tools have been integrated into a data lake. After that, off-the-shelf business analytics services provide simple but powerful interactive visualizations and analysis capabilities. With relatively little training, end users can create their own reports and dashboards; yet, it remains challenging to convince all stakeholders of the business value of investing in a more digital project management environment.

Prescriptive Capabilities: Real-Time Feedback on and Improvement Suggestions for Project Risk Registers

When entering a project risk, the author receives instant feedback on the quality of the risk description, including suggestions on how to close gaps in the risk description. The system helps project managers and product owners to describe project risks right the first time during risk identification workshops so that other stakeholders, such as sponsors and review committees, can effectively act upon them and ensure that risk descriptions can serve as a learning base in future projects.

Cognitive Capabilities: Auto-Generated Project Risk Registers

Based on the characteristics of past projects—their documented outcomes and learnings, evaluated risk and problem registers, their product family, served markets and other aspects—the data analytics system supports project managers by generating prefilled project risk registers. They are intended to replace copy and paste lists from previous projects, serving as starting points for risk identification workshops and highlighting possible lessons learned.

Question 4: How do we get hybrid intelligence to work?

We believe that enhanced ML and AI capabilities will add significant value to our organizations, unlocking both innovation and efficiency gains. Conversely, we often observe how we struggle to extract value from much more basic digitalization activities, such as ERP or CRM system deployments, or streamlining digital workflows through RPA. We call this the "maturity paradox," where we expect leaps in digital capabilities in our organizations while often observing the opposite. One important aspect here is, of course, the established wisdom that digitalization projects are never digitalization projects, but organizational change projects with a more or less ambitious IT component.

In addition, we suggest asking an additional question: How do we get hybrid intelligence to work? Hybrid intelligence describes the idea that computers are good at some things, and humans are good at other things. Basic examples are: humans are good at intuitively reality checking nonsense associations in our data (a popular exercise in most statistics classes—the divorce rate in Maine tracks nicely with per capita margarine consumption, for example), while algorithms can also challenge our own illusory associations (i.e., biases, if consciously and carefully developed for such a purpose). In order to make the best use of both, we must learn how to integrate the capabilities of both into our decision-making processes. Some people also call this the new "collective intelligence" of computers and humans. The two most important tasks to accomplish are (1) creating interpretability of analytical products and (2) interactivity between the two systems of computers and humans, described as follows:

1. **Interpretability:** Interpretability is an awkward one-word way of saying: The result of my technical analysis must be intuitively understandable by the decision maker. This is not an old problem. Talk to anyone in the intelligence community and you will hear many fascinating stories about the disconnects between (human) analysts and the (human) customers of their analytical products. Introducing computers into the equation does not make things easier. We often get this challenge the wrong way around: Decision makers must be educated to understand the beautiful and rich probability density function our model created after investing significant amounts of blood, sweat, and tears. While training decision makers to do new tricks is always desirable, we should also ask this question in the very early stages of designing our new analytical capabilities: How should we present the results so that our intended target audience can integrate them seamlessly into their existing decision-making structures? What are the minimum amounts of change and training absolutely required, and how can we best deliver them as parts of the development of our digitalization campaign?

2. **Interactivity:** Being able to play with models generates significant value for decision makers, including increased trust in its results. It allows users to, for example, vary input parameters to explore sensitivities; lets them change important modeling assumptions and observe the effects; or even adapt aspects of the model on the fly, for example, by changing weights in optimization functions. Another aspect is that interactivity opens up the door to creating a much easier cocreation experience, where decision makers become part of the modeling team. This drastically increases not only their understanding and trust, but also the quality of the modeling as it allows for a much closer interaction between modelers and decision makers.

Question 5: What is our human capability gap and how do we close it?

Last but not least, and maybe least surprising, we encounter a paradox surrounding the human capabilities of advanced digitalization: We talk, sometimes a lot, about now being the time to push a digitalization agenda and deploy advanced data analytics frameworks. We may even talk about how that affects our organizations and customers. However, we talk surprisingly little about how we can firmly integrate this goal into our core innovation and organizational development processes. So, the last question we want to discuss is: What is our digitalization capability gap and how do we close it? The two main aspects are people and processes:

1. **People:** What are the roles and how do we staff them to drive the development and adoption of advanced digital capabilities in our organization? Part of this question involves understanding existing roles and how they change as we prioritize digitalization. This is nothing new and arguably something that every organization has already done and has some experience with. Nevertheless, it is important to actively drive the evolution of roles instead of reacting in response to issues. Additionally, advanced data analytics capabilities will place much more emphasize on roles that thus far only have existed in the context such as machine learning ops (MLOps) responsibilities.

2. **Process:** Advanced data analytics capabilities must be integrated into existing organizational and innovation processes, but there are also specific development challenges that mean that organizations must create structured data analytics development processes. This is critical in order to ensure that advanced digitalization processes focus on the value they deliver to the organization and enable the organization to explore a range of options fast and at a reasonable cost.

AI is the answer if, and only if, your biggest problem is making better use of data. Advancing a digitalization agenda requires commitment, financial resources, and a very clear understanding of what the added business value is of what we are trying to do. Even articulating this value proposition will require attention and investment.

Against that backdrop, we have to ask ourselves this question: where does digitalization stand in the context of the other innovation and efficiency challenges our organization faces?

What we have seen is that organizations are successful even if they do not necessarily have a digitalization strategy but a strategy that also reflects their digitalization objectives. We believe the difference is important: Because the promises are big and the job is hard, it is easy to get carried away with a digitalization strategy that pursues an aggressive goal of more digitalization. Digitalization is not a goal in itself, but a means to an end. Only if we learn to leverage digitalization synergistically with other strategic initiatives will we reap its full benefits.

Acknowledgments

The authors thank Karim Meaouia, CEO of CK&CO, for his thoughtful comments on the manuscript. We also gratefully acknowledge the work of our graduate students, which has informed this article, including Laurids Mikkelsen, Simon Olt, Furkan Simsek, and Pelle Willumsen.

About the Authors

Josef Oehmen, PhD, MBA, is an Associate Professor at the Technical University of Denmark (DTU). His research focuses on designing and managing large-scale (systems) engineering programs, specifically how to deal with risk, uncertainty, and ignorance. He is the founder and coordinator of the RiskLab at DTU (http://risklab.dtu.dk). Prior to DTU, Josef worked at MIT and ETH Zurich (where he also earned his PhD).

Udo Hielscher, MBA, is Director and Corporate Process Owner Project Management at Bosch. One of his fields of focus is the digitalization of project management. Prior to his current assignment, Udo acted in different functions in the Bosch group, including Program Manager for a Bosch Europe Innovation Program, Postmerger Integration Manager and PMO lead at Bosch Solar Energy, as well as Team Lead at Tenovis. Udo holds a degree in electrical engineering from the University of Stuttgart and an MBA from the University of Applied Sciences in Mainz.

The Why of Digital Transformation

MARTIN REEVES AND ADAM JOB

We live in an age in which technology is increasingly crucial to developing and sustaining a competitive advantage: Seven of the world's 10 most valuable companies rely primarily on digital platforms, compared to two just 10 years ago. It is no wonder then that of the Fortune Future 50 companies—an annual ranking of firms according to their predicted future robust growth—about 50% originate from the technology sector and many others employ digital technology intensively (Reeves & Martinez, 2021).

For non-digitally native firms, this creates an imperative for digital transformation to preempt disruption. Indeed, such firms have embarked upon major change efforts, especially after the fillip to digital business models delivered by the COVID-19 pandemic. However, evidence indicates that more than two-thirds of digital transformations are unsuccessful (Forth et al., 2020). This is perhaps not surprising, given the depth and breadth of change involved and the array of new capabilities required.

For many companies, adopting digital technology is driven by a desire to catch up with peers or adopt best practices rather than as a means to achieve a competitive advantage. In this article, we explore how leveraging learnings from biology can help you succeed by framing digitalization as a way of creating adaptive advantage in a dynamic and uncertain environment.

Expanding our Definition of the Company

A company is often thought of as a sort of machine—an apparatus designed by humans, combining simple mechanisms, such as gears, pulleys, and levers, to perform a repetitive task predictably and efficiency. When thinking of the firm in this way, it is natural to aim to leverage a digital transformation to increase the execution efficiency of today's tasks within today's organizational context.

However, in the uncertain and dynamic business environment of today it may be more appropriate to think of firms as biological organisms, which evolve in response to changing conditions to ensure survival and advantage and to frame digital technology as a means to this end. Accordingly, the key question becomes: How can digital technology be used to confer adaptive advantage—the ability to learn, adapt, and thrive under changing conditions more effectively than rivals?

Perception, Action, and Sociality

Estonian biologist Jakob von Uexküll first framed the idea that an organism does not perceive the environment as it is, but rather a skewed version of it constrained by the organism's sense organs (Uexküll, 1909). He called such a partial view of the world an "umwelt" (Uexküll, 1934/2010). For example, a tick, which does not have eyes, perceives the world by sensing gradients of the butyric acid given off by the sweat glands of its mammalian hosts. When it senses high concentrations, it drops off its leaf, and if it is lucky enough to fall on a passing animal (which it knows by using its keen sense of temperature), it feels its way toward a hairless spot to attach and feed. In other words, organisms use their sensing capacities to create an updateable model of the world that is the basis for both action and learning how to act more effectively. This idea can be extended to cover not only perception but also cognition—the ability to make sense of signals and sociality and the ability to communicate and collaborate.

In some respects, humans are no different: Our worldview is limited by our five senses, by the things we can and cannot do, and by our capacity for communication with others. We do not spend a lot of time thinking about navigating electrical gradients, flying, or reading the minds of animals, because we cannot do those things unaided. However, there are also some important differences between humans and other mammals. As humans, we can be aware that our worldview is not complete or objective; we can deliberately shape it by learning, moving within the environment, or refocusing our senses and thoughts; we can use technology to enhance our senses and capabilities; and we can use our imagination to conceive that which does not yet exist (Reeves & Fuller, 2020). Furthermore, we can act socially to influence the worldviews of others, either by directly communicating new ideas or by manipulating the shared context, thus shaping the stimuli that others receive.

Implications for Digital Transformation

This framing can help us see the bigger picture of how technology can make companies fitter in new and ever-changing business environments. Beyond merely executing today's processes more efficiently, technology can also reshape how we sense and act on information. In particular, we can digitally transform to competitively enhance our organization's powers of perception and cognition; its capability to conceive novel ideas; and its ability to put these into action, both individually and in collaboration with others. Specifically, we can use technology to:

> **Extend the senses of the organization.** Technology expands our ability to capture signals beyond the traditional boundaries of the organization. For example, many leading technology companies have built massive digital ecosystems that give them access to proprietary data from a wide range of suppliers, customers, and other external sources (Pidun et al., 2019). Sensors and Internet of Things (IoT) technology can also

increase sensing ability by capturing new sources of data. These data, particularly if they reveal surprising or unknown patterns, can also serve as the spark that triggers a process of imagination (Reeves & Fuller, 2019).

Create connected digital learning loops. Traditionally, organizational learning was bounded by the rate at which individual human decision makers could learn from and act on information. With the advancement of artificial intelligence (AI), companies are now capable of learning and acting at algorithmic speed. Competing on the rate of learning is becoming a new basis for competition. To achieve this, data systems must be connected to AI algorithms, which in turn feed decision engines that can act without human intervention—and those actions create new data, forming an integrated learning loop (Reeves & Whitaker, 2020). For example, Netflix's recommendation platform captures granular consumer behavior; analyzes it at scale; and produces automated, personalized recommendations that evolve over time.

Focus humans and algorithms on their respective areas of strength. Algorithms can identify patterns in data much more quickly and powerfully than humans can. By delegating these tasks to machines, humans can focus on leveraging their own unique cognitive abilities such as imagining new possibilities that do not yet exist (Bailey et al., 2019). For example, Amazon has autonomized routine decisions for inventory management and pricing under a philosophy known as "Hands Off the Wheel," refocusing human talent on coming up with new ideas such as the company's Amazon Go stores. New human-algorithm interfaces will also be required to make these very different styles of cognition work together synergistically (Kantrowitz, 2020). We might call this the "bionic organization," which again expands possibilities for competing on the rate of learning.

Facilitate communication among brains. For new ideas to reach their potential, they must spread from one person to many, which allows them to be acted upon and evolve. Technology can be used to help understand and accelerate the spread of ideas throughout an organization. For example, metadata on people's interactions can inform a network map, which can be used to identify and reinforce brokers who bridge different functions or groups and who may thus be effective transmitters of new ideas.

Facilitate cooperation. Even if ideas are widely spread, that may not be enough to create alignment and action. Collective action involves changing the beliefs of many individual actors (Reeves & Torres, 2020). Technology is no panacea here, but when harnessed correctly, digital platforms help scale and accelerate collective understanding and action.

For example, Wikipedia has enabled millions of users to contribute and organize their knowledge into a freely available, comprehensive digital encyclopedia. Business ecosystems effectively enable their orchestrators to compete on their ability to coordinate with others and, given the network effectives involved, this can create a durable basis for advantage.

Diagnose system health to overcome planetary and social limits.
Businesses do not operate in a vacuum; environmental and social challenges are increasingly relevant to businesses in all sectors. In the short run this creates constraints but in the long run it is likely that these constraints will create new bases for advantage. Digital technology cannot only facilitate individual and collective contributions to social and ecological challenges but also the realization of forms of sustainability advantage.

There is one area, however, where technology will not help: setting the purpose and ethics of a business. Only humans can decide the ends to which technology and the corporation are applied. Each company must determine why it exists and how it creates the intersection of capabilities, aspirations, and social needs—this also must guide transformation efforts in addition to the competitive issues described above.

The Power of Biological Organizations

The outlined technology agenda fits with a broader strategic agenda of thriving amid uncertainty and complexity, in marked contrast to traditional static approaches to strategy. This approach may be uncomfortable to many leaders trained to maximize scale, short-run efficiency, and financial returns, rather than learning or social contribution. Leaders can reshape their digital transformation efforts to tap into this new biological paradigm by asking themselves several pivotal questions:

- Do our efforts expand the perceptive power of the organization?
- Do our efforts enhance the sensemaking capability of the organization?
- Do our efforts enhance the imaginative capabilities of the organization?
- Do our efforts enhance the learning capability of the organization?
- Do the roles of human and algorithmic cognition combine synergistically to enhance learning?
- Do our efforts tap into the collaborative power of external ecosystems?
- Are we using technology to increase social contribution and create

sustainability advantage?

- In aggregate, does our deployment of digital technology merely reinforce status quo processes or status quo gaps with competitors, or can it create competitive advantage through superior perception, cognition, sociality, and translation into action?

Embracing a broader biological conception of the firm will help leaders to not only see technology as an end in itself, but rather as a means for enhancing the ability of the organization to learn and compete in a changing and unpredictable context.

A version of this article previously appeared on bcg.com (Reeves & Whitaker, 2020)

References

Bailey, A., Reeves, M., Whitaker, K., & Hutchinson, R. (2019). *The company of the future.* BCG. https://www.bcg.com/en-us/publications/2019/company-of-the-future

Forth, P., Reichert, T., de Labier, R., & Chakraborty, S. (2020). *Flipping the odds of digital transformation success.* BCG. https://www.bcg.com/publications/2020/increasing-odds-of-success-in-digital-transformation

Kantrowitz, A. (2020). *How Amazon automated work and put its people to better use.* Harvard Business Review online. https://hbr.org/2020/09/how-amazon-automated-work-and-put-its-people-to-better-use.

Pidun, U., Reeves, M., & Schussler, M. (2019). *Do you need a business ecosystem?* BCG. https://www.bcg.com/publications/2019/do-you-need-business-ecosystem

Reeves, M., & Fuller, J. (2019). *Competing on imagination.* BCG. https://bcghendersoninstitute.com/competing-on-imagination-22984574aa48

Reeves, M., & Fuller, J. (2020). *We need imagination now more than ever.* Harvard Business Review. https://hbr.org/2020/04/we-need-imagination-now-more-than-ever

Reeves, M., & Martinez, D. Z. (2021). *The 2021 Fortune Future 50,* https://www.bcg.com/publications/2021/fortune-future-50-companies-show-growth

Reeves, M., & Torres, R. (2020). *In sync: Unlocking collective action in a connected world.* BCG.

https://www.bcg.com/publications/2020/collective-action-in-a-connected-world

Reeves, M., & Whitaker, K. (2020). *The why of digital transformation.* BCG. https://www.bcg.com/publications/2020/the-power-of-digital-transformation

Uexküll, J. von (1909). *Umwelt und innenwelt der tiere.* J. Springer.

Uexküll, J. von (1934/2010). *A foray into the worlds of animals and humans with a theory of meaning.* University of Minnesota Press.

About the Authors

Martin Reeves is a Managing Director and Senior Partner in BCG's San Francisco office and Chairman of the BCG Henderson Institute, BCG's vehicle for exploring ideas from beyond the world of business, which have implications for business strategy management. He is the coauthor of *The*

Imagination Machine (HBR Press, 2021), *Your Strategy Needs a Strategy* (HBR Press, 2015), and the *Inspiring the Next Game* series (DeGruyter 2021).

Adam Job is a Project Leader at the BCG Henderson Institute based in BCG's Frankfurt office.

How to Design and Unlock the Strategic Value of Your Transformation Office

ANDREW SCHUSTER, KARSTEN KUHRMEIER, JULIE MCCLEAN, AND SAMUEL POWNALL

16

For many organizations, new approaches to managing transformation are needed to maximize their value. Increasingly, organizations are turning toward the transformation office (TO) to drive their transformations.

PwC and Project Management Institute (PMI) embarked on joint research to understand how leading organizations successfully drive transformation through the transformation office (TO). Our worldwide survey of over 4,000 project management practitioners, 2,600 project management offices (PMOs), and 700 TOs, shows that organizations with mature TO functions go beyond a tactical perspective of projects, at once building the links among individual projects and the organization's strategy and prioritizing initiatives that will drive long-term success. In addition, effective prioritization allows better C-suite support and change without overburdening the organization.

Our findings have been developed using a first-of-its-kind Transformation Maturity Index, an index created by PwC and PMI that measures fundamental TO activities, which drive successful transformation. This index has allowed us to identify five key areas of focus when designing the TO to maximize its impact and explore examples of best practices from leading organizations identified in our research. These areas are:

1. Accelerating TO maturity and its strategic impact,
2. Managing project and transformation talent,
3. Measuring project success with an outcome-focused model,
4. Technology implementation that supports transformation management, and
5. Adapting for the future.

Leading organizations will be referred to throughout this article as the "Top 10 Percent." These high performers have driven positive transformation outcomes for their organizations, which have been more than twice as likely to perform better in a range of key performance indicators: revenue growth; customer acquisition; customer satisfaction; and environmental, social, and governance (ESG) metrics.

The majority of the Top 10 Percent have corporate-level governance offices such as an enterprise PMO (ePMO). This underlines the benefit of designing a TO or an ePMO, one that has a centralized, organization-wide approach. These offices support governance, best practices, and project/program alignment across departments and functions, helping to ensure transformations are generating value for the organization according to its goals.

Accelerating TO Maturity and its Strategic Impact

PwC and PMI's maturity index measures fundamental TO activities that drive successful transformation. The more frequent the activity, the greater the maturity of the TO. We measured levels of activity against 23 specific elements of maturity, across the following five dimensions:

Governance: How often a TO provides project visibility, measures performance, and supports decision-making;

Integration and alignment: How effectively the TO engages stakeholders, coordinates projects, and integrates TO processes across business functions to provide support ensures strategic alignment;

Processes: How often a TO reviews and adapts project management tools, methodologies, and practices to different projects and teams;

Technology and data: How often a TO uses the latest project and program management tools and uses data to enhance decision-making; and

People: How often a TO invests in activities related to performance management, developing, and upskilling talent.

To accelerate the maturity of the TO, C-suite support is vital. Our research highlights that C-suite support and providing the TO with a seat at the table within the governance structure, is a key characteristic of the most mature organizations. Only with a mandate from senior leadership is a TO able to effectively drive action and remove obstacles, allowing it to implement a strong governance structure that can challenge both downwards and upwards, and encourage stakeholders and employees to take responsibility for driving forward the organization's strategy.

Senior leaders will also be able to take advantage of the TO's knowledge of projects across its portfolio—knowledge that is crucial for aligning and prioritizing the portfolio to business strategy. While 73% of the Top 10 Percent have a C-suite level role that represents PMOs, only 47% of global organizations have this formal relationship in place. Establishing a representative of the TO in the C-suite is a key enabler for transformation success (Figure 1).

The Project Management/ Transformation Office and the C-Suite	Global Top 10% (n = 230)	Global Bottom 10% (n = 239)
Agree that the C-suite understands and appreciates their value	94%	37%
Agree that the C-suite in their organization them to be a strategic partner	94%	34%
Agree that the C-suite supports and demonstrates commitment to their success	94%	36%

Figure 1. C-suite support is a key feature of the most mature PMOs and TOs.

Managing Project and Transformation Talent

It is key during the TO design phase to consider how it will attract, onboard, and develop talent in order to emulate the most mature organizations. The delivery of complex transformations is people driven, and the TO has a crucial role in developing a culture that supports effective communication, collaboration, and motivates people to create positive change.

The Top 10 Percent organizations demonstrate an equal commitment to their people as they do to strong governance, considering how they can help develop skills such as leadership, flexibility, and strategic acumen. By taking the same approach, newly designed TOs cannot only create a team of changemakers that support the organization's vision—they will also attract skilled employees to a role that offers quick development and an opportunity to have a strategic impact on the business. A modern approach to talent management is needed—one that recognizes that project manager capabilities need to evolve beyond a focus solely on scope, budget, and schedule to have a strategic impact.

The most important capabilities to have in a TO are those that enable a human and a strategic approach to project management. PwC's report, Who is *The Modern Project Manager?* (PwC, 2021), shows that a future-ready project influencer has an increasing focus on influencing outcomes, building relationships, and achieving the strategic goals of their organizations. This approach is supported by the latest research by PwC and PMI, which found that the five most important skills deemed critical to successful project delivery and transformation are a mix of people skills and commercial awareness (Figure 2).

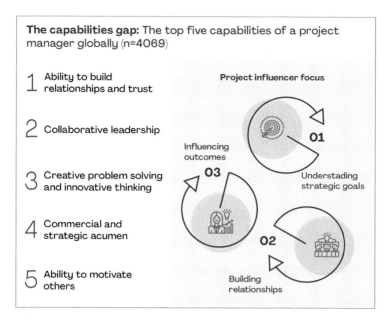

The capabilities gap: The top five capabilities of a project manager globally (n=4069)

1 Ability to build relationships and trust

2 Collaborative leadership

3 Creative problem solving and innovative thinking

4 Commercial and strategic acumen

5 Ability to motivate others

Project influencer focus

01

Influencing outcomes

03

Understading strategic goals

02

Building relationships

Figure 2. The capabilities gap: The top five capabilities of a project manager globally.

Recruitment and onboarding can be used as an opportunity to find and emphasize these capabilities and behaviors. As highlighted in *Narrowing the Talent Gap* report published with PMI, the public perception of the project profession is a major barrier to recruitment; project managers are often viewed as tactical troubleshooters rather than strategic partners in the organization (PMI, 2021). Fifty-four percent of organizations in our survey describe project managers as "schedulers" and less than one-fifth chose phrases, such as "flexible," "creative," and "realizing visions," compared to over one-third of the Top 10 Percent. TOs have an important role to play in improving the image of the profession by clearly demonstrating the strategic creativity involved in the role. This will help organizations gain a competitive advantage in the race for transformation management talent.

TOs can gain an additional advantage by designing a clear learning and development strategy for its employees, one that is linked to the TO's objectives and the wider organizational strategy. Alongside core technical and digital skills, organizations need to consider how to develop the key skills of the modern project manager as highlighted in Figure 2.

The impact of training and development should be tracked to encourage continued investment in the skills needed to enable successful transformations. However, only 22% of organizations have processes in place to monitor the use and progress of training. This suggests the majority of organizations have no evidence of whether learning and development programs are actually improving capabilities—and in turn will be unable to demonstrate to executives they are getting returns from investment, which feeds the lack of strategic prioritization. This needs to change, so organizations have incentives to review and evolve approaches to training and can demonstrate its positive impact on business outcomes.

Measuring Project Success With an Outcome-Focused Model

Tracking desired business outcomes is a crucial part of successful transformations; it helps maintain momentum and provides critical information to senior leaders, especially when it comes to making trade-off decisions and reprioritizing a portfolio. For measurement to be impactful, TOs need to use their strategic acumen to align measures with the organization's key objectives. Key questions to answer when implementing measurement are:

- How are the initiatives within the transformation program supporting the organization's strategy?
- Which organizational key performance indicators (KPIs) is the transformation program aiming to impact (e.g., customer satisfaction or operational efficiencies)?
- Which stakeholders need to be involved in the development of performance metrics and how can the TO involve the C-suite and/or strategic leads in the development of these metrics?
- How can the TO use digital solutions to make portfolio performance easily accessible so it can support informed decision-making?

Answering these questions can help support an outcome-focused model of measurement—an approach centered on tracking the most meaningful outcomes the organization is hoping to achieve from their transformation strategy.

However, many organizations are still overly reliant on the iron triangle and, while these are still important measures, not considering value creation beyond if a project is in scope, budget, and on time will not provide a clear view if a transformation is moving the organization in the right direction. In contrast, the Top 10 Percent maintain transformation momentum toward its long-term ambitions by focusing more on key outcomes, for example, customer satisfaction, operational efficiencies, and alignment to the wider organizational strategy.

The first step is to design measures so they capture the key benefits the transformation is trying to achieve. These will be unique to each organization; therefore, it is important that measures not be developed in a silo else they risk measuring factors that are not relevant to the organization. The Top 10

Percent take this collaborative approach to measuring; they are much more likely to engage with a wider range of stakeholders across the organization, including customers, PMOs, and auditors. This focuses outcome measures on meaningful outcomes that are most relevant in the organization and sector.

Many organizations can struggle to get the C-suite involved in the development of measures. By doing so, however, it is much more likely that measures put in place will be impactful and relevant to the organization's long-term goals. Our research found that, in 2020, more mature organizations were more likely to have shifted their approach to measurement in response to the disruption of the COVID-19 pandemic—76% of the Top 10 Percent aligned performance of the TO to organizational strategy and KPIs (versus 56% globally). This was supported by greater engagement with the C-suite; the Top 10 Percent were more likely to have engaged the C-suite in the development of metrics (57% versus 34% globally).

The TO should consider how it can use technology, such as strategy execution management technology and benefit realization tools, to help capture more metrics beyond the iron triangle. Our report, *Measuring What Matters*, copublished with PMI, highlights how organizations that utilize technology find it easier to measure project and program impacts, and consider their PMOs to be more successful than those that don't use technology to track measures (PMI, 2022).

Technology Implementation That Supports Transformation Management

Getting out of the starting gate quickly helps to accelerate transformations. TOs that take advantage of modern technological solutions can minimize time spent on developing new processes and methodologies, instead getting straight into the business of leading change and generating value.

TOs with a digital mindset can help drive the implementation of tools that strengthen governance as well as reporting *and* supporting the delivery of transformational change. Tools that focus on collaboration, improving project visibility, and knowledge sharing can support leadership's ability to make informed and quicker decisions through real-time insights. Automation tools can support delivery, increase quality, and significantly free up project resources. Consider how technology can support:

- Coordination and collaboration with stakeholders;
- Improving the visibility of projects to facilitate strategic decision-making;
- Managing governance, risk, and compliance more effectively; and
- Improving knowledge management, sharing, and transfer.

A key advantage of technology is freeing up project managers' time from repetitive tasks so they can spend more time collaborating with the organization on strategy and change management. Using technology to help evolve the project manager's role into one that has more of a strategic focus has the additional benefit of making the role more attractive, helping to ease some of the recruitment challenges organizations face.

It is also important for organizations to consider how they will compete in 5 to 10 years in a landscape significantly impacted by emerging technologies. Our survey showed that 49% of global respondents think artificial intelligence (AI) will be used by their organization in five years' time, yet only 21% are currently using AI to improve the management of technologies. The TO should be open to embracing new technologies as they emerge, even considering how future solutions can be implemented during the design phase. Fast adoption of new technology can help the TO react quickly to change and remain relevant.

It is important that organizations and TOs consider how they can build trust with stakeholders and users when implementing technology. PwC's *Global Digital Trust Insights* report shows that organizations are shifting their cybersecurity approach from a narrow, operational focus, to developing trust and business growth, but highlights that CEOs still need to do more to create a digitally proficient culture (PwC, 2023). This supports results from our survey, which found that 37% of organizations think lack of prioritization from the C-suite is a key culture challenge to implementing technology, and one-third say there is a lack of technology skills among project teams.

Communicating openly about the purposes and benefits of new technology and building trust with employees are crucial to encouraging digital ways of working; our research highlights that these need to be supported through training and coaching in the use of digital tools to improve the digital skills of project teams. While TOs play an important role in promoting a digital culture, they will need support from the C-suite. TOs can help generate this support by raising awareness of the strategic value of technology especially when it is used to support fast and effective decision-making. Much of the responsibility, however, lies with senior leadership; they need to understand that a lasting competitive advantage in the current market is reliant on having the right technology strategy in place.

Fit for the Future

Leading organizations demonstrated the benefits of TO maturity by helping their organizations adapt quickly during the COVID-19 pandemic. The top 10% were much more effective than the bottom 10% in supporting the acceleration of new ways of working, enhancing risk assessments and migration, and using the disruption of the pandemic as an opportunity to demonstrate their ability to deliver value.

As hybrid working environments become more common, it is vital to establish strong communication processes between the TO and the C-suite, so decision makers still have the information they need to make informed decisions without necessarily needing to be on the ground. Mature organizations reacted during the COVID-19 pandemic by strengthening their relationship with the C-suite and improving alignment, using the following steps:

- Improving communication and transparency around projects, including meaningful milestones, issues, value, and impact;
- Aligning the priorities and performance of the PMO to organizational strategy and KPIs;
- Working with C-suite champions to drive change; and
- Coaching/mentoring senior leaders to better support them in being executive sponsors.

By investing in the maturity of the TO, organizations can increase their ability to react to the inevitable disruption and change that will occur during its implementation.

Call to Action

- Establish C-suite support for the TO to help move it beyond the execution of projects to a place where it can help inform and drive the organization's strategy.
- Develop measures focused on key outcomes of the transformation strategy. Collaborate with the C-suite to ensure that measurement is aligned with and supports the organization's overall strategic goals.
- The impending talent shortage will place transformations and projects at risk of failure if organizations don't act quickly. Building winning capabilities needs to become a strategic priority, with a greater emphasis placed on more creative and effective hiring, retention, and upskilling strategies. Subcontracting the TO is another potential solution.
- Widespread digital upskilling and a cultural shift toward a digital mindset at the C-suite level and within the TO need to happen at pace.
- Hybrid working is set to become the norm; the TO needs to focus on how it can improve communication with the C-suite and teams delivering the transformation.

References

Project Management Institute (PMI). (2021). *Narrowing the talent gap.* https://www.pmi.org/learning/thought-leadership/narrowing-the-talent-gap

Project Management Institute (PMI). (2022). *Measuring what matters*. https://www.pmi.org/learning/thought-leadership/measuring-what-matters

PwC. (2021). *Who is the modern project manager?* https://www.pwc.com/m1/en/blogs/pdf/who-is-the-modern-project-manager.pdf

PwC. (2023). *Global digital trust insights report.* https://www.pwc.com/dti2023

About the Authors

Dr. Andrew Schuster is a Partner in PwC Canada's Transformation Risk and Advisory practice. He has over 30 years of international experience researching, designing, delivering, and reviewing major organizational transformation programs.

Karsten Kuhrmeier is a Transformation Risk & Advisory Director for PwC Canada, supporting clients with their complex transformation projects.

Julie McClean is the Head of Quantitative Research at PwC Research, PwC's Global Centre of Excellence for bespoke primary market research and insight.

Samuel Pownall is an Insight Consultant at PwC Research, where he specializes in primary research and thought leadership on the strategic implementation of transformation and project management.

Transformation in a Digital World

ROBIN SPECULAND

I t is not about having a digital strategy! It is about having a strategy in the digital world.

This is not just semantics—it's the difference between failure and success. Why? When you craft your strategy to compete in the digital world, you widen your strategic lens at a time when the winds of change blow harder and faster externally than they do internally. To future proof your strategy, you need to take into consideration broader perspectives such as inflation, geopolitical situations, changes in the labor market, and emerging technologies. Crafting a digital strategy limits many leadership teams' perspectives and dangerously narrows the focus.

A significant challenge we are seeing in many organizations is that they are struggling to move from the reacting to embedding stages in digital transformation (the third stage is strategic, where you create new revenue opportunities to greater customer value). Our latest research (Bridges Business Consultancy, 2022) reveals that 71% of individuals are in the first stage of digital maturity and only have the knowledge but not the skills to participate in a digital world. Transformation in a digital world requires not only redesigning your business model but also identifying the technologies and methodologies that need to be adopted to support and drive the creation of greater customer value. Leaders are responsible for identifying these and their impact as well as the most effective way to incorporate them into the organization. The initial investment involves a high CAPEX, with the return on investment initially coming from savings, then from the top line growth from new revenue opportunities.

Simultaneously, leaders need to also guide and lead the organization through the whole business model transformation, which typically impacts every part of the business. No wonder two-thirds of digital transformations are still failing (McKinsey & Company, 2021).

Why are organizations struggling to move from reacting to embedding? It is because many struggle to understand how all the different components of digital technology can be implemented. This issue was already surfacing in 2019 when it emerged in our research of over 1,800 leaders across North America, Europe, and Asia Pacific (Bridges Business Consultancy, 2019). From the research and client work, we identified the top three reasons why digital transformation fails: (1) senior leaders' reluctance to change their mindset, (2) the challenges of changing organizational culture, and (3) digital transformation success is not just about applying digital lipstick but transforming the whole business model.

Ticking Clock Model

To support leaders, we developed the *Digital Leadership Playbook* (Blain & Speculand, 2020) and the ticking clock model, which includes three strategic stages leaders need to consider and 11 operational steps. The three strategic stages are explained as follows and highlight many of the operational steps:

1. Future thinking: Establish a clear digital vision and develop a leadership growth and digital mindset.

The leadership needs to identify their digital vision by thinking about tomorrow, referred to as their "future thinking." This creates a digital vision that becomes the North Star, aligns the whole organization, and guides the creation of digital measures. The digital vision starts by recognizing that it's not technology disrupting your business but customers.

Future thinking also includes developing a leadership's digital mindset. This involves letting go of legacy leadership—also known as vertical leadership— as this requires that employees need to keep requesting permission and budgets from their leaders and attending meetings. Successful organizations in the digital world adopt horizontal leadership where they create an agile culture with empowered employees who can manage customer journeys horizontally and also leverage data.

Under the stewardship of Piyush Gupta, DBS Bank, for example, has been recognized as the best bank in the world for five years in a row. In 2014, the bank's transformation in a digital world began with the leadership team offsite where they discussed the implications of their new vision, which was to "make banking joyful." Joyful is not a word you typically associate with banking, but for DBS it created a passion to leverage technology to make banking invisible to their customers, hence enjoyable. The marketing slogan became "live more, bank less." Internally, this initially caused some confusion as to why the bank was asking customers to bank less, but it soon became apparent that it meant less time for customers conducting their banking because they used digital enablers.

2. Centricity around customers, culture, and operations: Identify the changes to your business model.

With the digital vision created, an organization then needs to examine centricity around its customers, culture, and operations. A key reason digital transformation fails is because leaders underestimate the impact on their business model. Becoming digitally driven frequently requires a whole business model transformation. It's not about tweaking or adjusting the business model or automation but rather a whole business model transformation, which starts with the customer.

Adopting digital methodologies, such as agile, design thinking, hackathons, and customer journey mapping, the organization revisits the value it provides customers and looks for ways to improve it by eliminating customer pain points and focusing on the job to be done. This is leading many organizations to shift from selling products to platforms. Consider how Apple doesn't just sell you a mobile product but engages you on their digital lifestyle platform, which includes messaging, music, apps, health, TV, and other value.

Centricity starts and ends with the customer (even for B2B businesses); it involves truly understanding customer needs and expectations through the use of data and digital technologies and methodologies such as AI and custom returning mapping.

It involves adopting agile, eliminating silos (as organizations transform from vertical to horizontal management), and empowering employees. Becoming digitally driven starts with the digital vision but is implemented from the ground upward, which is why the digital vision is vital. Simultaneously, the technology architecture needs to evolve to support the new business model.

DBS adopted these three strategic principles to drive the implementation of making banking joyful:

Become digital from the core. Create a rock-solid foundation of core systems the bank could build on and orchestrate a complete transformation of the bank from front to back office.

Embed ourselves in the customer journey. Make banking invisible by leveraging technology and adopting customer journey thinking throughout the organization, which drives toward becoming customer obsessed.

Create a 33,000-person start-up. Change the culture of the organization, recognizing that this is one of the most precarious areas of organizational transformation and ensure they take risks, operate in a nimble way, and have an energy similar to forming a start-up. A start-up culture mindset to DBS is defined as being:

- Agile,
- A learning organization,
- Customer obsessed,
- Data driven, and
- Open to experimentation.

3. Future proofing: Measure your digital strategy while becoming data driven and building business sustainability.

The leadership team needs to ensure continuality and sustainability. Transforming a whole business model transformation takes time, tenacity, dedication across the entire organization, and discipline, which many organizations often lack. A new strategy requires new measures to track the implementation and take corrective action as required. Many of the measures required in becoming digitally driven are new to organizations, such as value from digital customers, paperless workflow, and scalability, and as such require leaders to focus and pay attention to identify what to measure and how.

A critical part of transformation in a digital world is also building a data culture, where the organization shifts to using real-time data and data visualization to make decisions. This allows the organization to react faster to market and customer changes and to have what the Chinese company Haier calls "zero distance" between themselves and their customers. This means that customer inputs are in real time and driving the innovation.

Organizations that have transformed to a data-first culture don't allow slide deck presentations in meetings (as the data being presented are not in real time) and have spent considerable time and effort on defining the right data, how to capture it, use it, and protect it. The three strategic stages make the core of our Ticking Clock Model for transformation in the digital world.

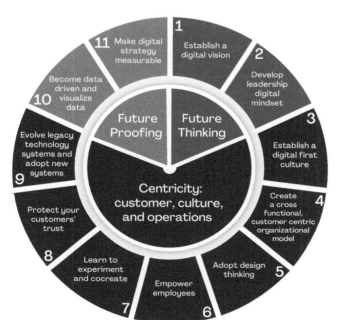

Figure 1. The Ticking Clock© Model. The outer circle highlights the 11 operational steps involved.

References

Blain, J., & Speculand, R. (2020). *Digital leadership playbook.* Bridges Business Consultancy. http://www.bridgesconsultancy.com/wp-content/uploads/2021/11/Digital-Leadership-Playbook-sample.pdf

Bridges Business Consultancy. (2019). *Digital leadership specialists.* www.bridgesconsultancy.com/digital-leadership-specialists

Bridges Business Consultancy. (2022). *Digital maturity index report 2022.* http://www.bridgesconsultancy.com/wp-content/uploads/2022/11/DMI-Report-2022.pdf

McKinsey & Company. (2021). *Losing from day one: Why even successful transformations fall short.* www.mckinsey.com/business-functions/people-and-organizational-performance/our-insights/successful-transformations

About the Author

Robin Speculand is a recognized pioneer and expert in strategy and digital implementation. He is driven to transform strategy implementation by inspiring global leaders to adopt a different mindset and approach. The founder of three companies, Robin is CEO of Bridges Business Consultancy International and co-founder of the Strategy Implementation Institute and Digital Leadership Specialists. A TEDx presenter and Thinkers50 nominee, he is a facilitator for IMD, Duke CE, and SMU. As a best-selling author, he has written six books, including his most recent, *World's Best Bank: A Strategic Guide to Digital Transformation,* and *Strategy Implementation Playbook: A Step-By-Step Guide.*

The Digital Transformation of Industrial Firms: What, Why, and How

ANNIKA STEIBER

18

New digital technologies are transforming every industry, and the digitization of almost every business process has triggered a broader digital transformation phenomenon across most industries. The challenge for firms is not to add a digital *touch* to current practices and products but to *fully exploit* digital technologies' transformative potential. However, with the increasing pace of technological development, the dilemma of large firms is that there is little evidence that industrial giants are the ones that ensure rapid technological change and rapid utilization of new techniques. The challenge for large firms is, therefore, not only to explore but to exploit new technologies and be able to make necessary business and operational model transformations.

Currently there is no commonly accepted definition for the term "digital transformation." Therefore, in this article digital transformation of a firm is defined as: "the firm uses new digital innovations to enable major business improvements" (Steiber et al., 2020, p. 800).

Digital Transformation Requires Changes to Social and Technical Systems

It is important to understand that a digital transformation must be viewed as a *sociotechnical and therefore complex phenomenon*, in which the digital transformation is a result of a change of both the technical and the social systems in the transforming organization. Researchers have known for decades that technological and management innovations are interdependent and strongly affect the final business outcome, which implies that only making changes in one of the two systems will not lead to major business improvements and, therefore, not be viewed as a true digital transformation of an organization.

Another aspect to consider is the degree of digital transformation of a company. The degree of business transformation is directly correlated to the business benefits potential (Venkatraman, 1994). The lowest level of business transformation would be to do only a localized exploitation of digital technologies, for example, digitalize the invoicing process in the financial department. The highest level of business transformation would be business scope redefinition or business model innovation. To transform an invoicing process versus the whole business model will of course have impacts on the final business benefits potential.

Currently, only a minority of large firms have managed to truly explore and exploit disruptive digital technologies and gain transformational effects from these on the business model level. This raises the following questions: Why do most firms struggle and even fail in their business transformations? What would contribute to large industrial firms' success in digitally transforming themselves on a business model level? What are the drivers and inhibitors for a successful transformation?

To answer these questions, companies are searching for blueprints, checklists, and success cases to learn from. However, the blueprints, checklists, and success cases on how to conduct a successful transformation are very few, if not non-existent. The reason for this is that any transformation is a result of changes in both the social and technical systems in an organization. This is the reason why a transformation demands a systemic approach in which multiple organizational components, such as leadership, organizational design, and more, need to be considered. When doing this, it is hard, if not impossible to just copy and paste the recipe from another company. Instead, the transforming company needs to understand the underlying principles behind the role model's change and then interpret and translate each of these principles to their own unique environment. Any transformation, therefore, requires the interpretation and translation work to be done by a core group of the transforming company. Furthermore, to change a social system includes changing the behaviors of people; therefore, any transforming organization needs to skillfully change how people will behave toward one another and toward external parties in the future.

Business Transformation Requires a Cultural Transformation

One model that includes both the social and technical systems of an organization is the framework by Schein (2010), shown in Table 1. Edgar Schein has been commonly called the father of the concept of corporate culture and is world famous for his extraordinary work and dedication to understanding the complex concept of corporate culture.

Table 1. Three-Tier Model of Culture (modified from Schein, 2010)

Artifacts	Visible structures and processes; observed behaviors
Espoused Values	Outspoken ideals, goals, aspirations; ideologies and rationalizations
Tacit Assumptions	Taken-for-granted, unconscious beliefs, assumptions of the world

The first two levels are what the outsider can readily see (artifacts) and hear (espoused values). Here the first level, artifacts, could represent the technical system, whereas the first (observed behaviors), second (espoused values), and third levels (underlying assumptions of the world) are parts of the social system.

The content of an organization's culture—just like most other things in our lives—has a virtual or cyber representation that is just as tangible and may be more powerful than the shape of a building or the posters on the walls. The observer might not see or hear the third layer—the underlying assumptions (also part of the social system)—yet we know they are there; this layer, once we start to understand it, generally explains any inconsistencies we perceive between the top two layers—artifacts and espoused values.

The Transformation of GE Appliances (GEA)

The GEA case represents an interesting opportunity to study a transformation of a 100-year-old American industrial firm on the level of business model transformation.

When it was sold to the Haier Group in 2016, GE Appliances (GEA) had been part of General Electric (GE) for a long time. Before the sale, GEA had experienced stagnant growth and loss of market share while adhering to the parent company's culture and ways of doing business. The focus was "doing no harm" and "increasing short-term profits" through cost-efficiency and control, and the organization could be characterized as a closed system with bureaucratic top-down structure. In 2021, five years after the acquisition, the company had become the fastest growing appliance company in the United States and had been named the "Smart Appliance Company of the Year" by IoT Breakthrough for four consecutive years. The company goal was now to become number one in the North American market. The culture had changed from believing in a bureaucratic top-down organization to a networked organization consisting of previously existing and new smaller, user-focused businesses (microenterprises), supported by the previous operational functions.

An Analysis of GEA's Transformation

The story of GEA highlights clearly how the transformation was, and is, supported by the CEO's conscious focus on influencing and changing all three tiers of the company's corporate culture: the underlying assumptions, espoused values, and artifacts (the technical system and behavior). This holistic and conscious approach ultimately led to a transformation of the whole company in a relatively short time.

In 2016, GEA's CEO, Kevin Nolan, was already frustrated with the parent (GE) company's mindset and way of doing business, which was deeply rooted in valuing efficiency, reliability, and profit margin. This frustration finally led to the launch of an innovative new way of working with R&D, labeled "FirstBuilt," in 2014. In 2016, after the company was acquired, Nolan's own assumptions were verified and supported by the new owner, Haier. Haier's management model, RenDanHeYi, consisted of principles that mirrored Nolan's own assumptions of how to run the company. After being appointed the new CEO of GEA, Nolan acted as an *intentional value changemaker* and decided to use RenDanHeYi as a set of management principles to aim for. Next, he communicated the new espoused values, such as becoming number one in North America, the user is the new boss, and leadership in digital technologies, to everyone in the organization. He then initiated a change of the organization's artifacts by transforming product lines into microenterprises (independent businesses), delegating decision-making power to the new business owners, and altering the compensation model so it better reflects true value creation. Part of the transformation of artifacts was the new use of digital technologies, which changed the way of working both upstream and downstream. From a digital technology perspective, GEA found in the Zero Distance philosophy a key driver to accelerate its transition from an *analogic-hardware-centric company* to a *digital-software-enable ecosystem*. The digital transformation was an intentional intervention, bringing the entire supply chain under one single digital platform, called Brilliant Factory, or CosmoPlat. A similar intervention was made in the consumer-facing space, expanding and continuously improving the connected appliances offerings under the brand SmartHQ, which also allowed two-way communication between consumers and the company. Under the SmartHQ platform, consumers have digital control over their appliances and can digitally connect with service teams, purchase parts, or manage entire properties. The digital transformation has enabled GEA to get closer to consumers to serve them better.

By behaving according to the new espoused values, communicating them weekly to everyone in the company, as well as changing the artifacts—such as structure, processes, compensation model, and digital platforms—the cultural transformation was strengthened, even if not everyone totally understood or bought into the underlying assumptions behind the new espoused values or ways of managing GEA. Potential resistance was handled by involving key stakeholders one level at a time (starting from the top and working on one level at a time) in the organization and transparently discussing the need for change, the new set of management assumptions, as well as how to best change. Key stakeholders were asked to suggest potential solutions for the new way of working and present them to the executive team, consisting of only three people who met weekly in a so called "pulse meeting," with the purpose of taking the temperature of the transformation process. The new set of assumptions, however, were not debatable such as the belief in aligning the whole organization toward the needs of users and that users are "your new boss." Some leaders found it hard to accept their new role; however, by allowing open discussions with, and consistent and clear communication from the executive team, most senior leaders finally accepted the changes in their roles. Consequently, today, the senior leadership team is aligned and shares the same assumptions on how to manage the company, as well as the communicated espoused values and changes in fundamental artifacts.

As a next step, employees reporting to the senior leaders were educated and encouraged to buy into the new assumptions and the communicated espoused values as well as new artifacts. By observing the top leadership behavior and listening to their consistent message about the importance of change as well as of success stories due to the change, employees in the organization started altering their own assumptions and, consequently, behavior.

This process demanded more than one year and, in 2021, the company was still working on integrating the new management assumptions. Externally, customer and stakeholder reactions to the initiatives of the organization also played an important role. The CEO's speeches at world conferences, such as the Drucker Forum, highlighted that GEA's transformation was not only of interest to external stakeholders, but it was admired and perceived as something in line with the new digital economy. This had a positive effect on GEA employees' confidence in their continued business transformation, which further strengthened the change process.

In the GEA case, the acquisition by Haier and the exposure to the RenDanHeYi philosophy provided the new CEO with a direction in his business transformation of the company. The altered assumptions, values, and artifacts, agreed on by the new CEO and the owner Haier, generated a new sociotechnical system in the organization. GEA's new management system, the GEA Way, mirrors RenDanHeYi used by the parent company, but is locally adjusted for the unique conditions for GEA in North America.

Conclusions

A digital transformation of a corporation is a systemic and complex task as it affects both the social and technical systems of an organization. By using Edgar Schein's framework for corporate culture, including three tiers, underlying assumptions, espoused values, and artifacts, a company can transform its organization and its people in a systemic way. In addition to what has been discussed in this article, a transformation process should not be viewed as a finite process but as an infinite one, with no end. In today's economy, every organization needs to constantly change and sometimes (with an increasing frequency) also conduct transformational changes of its business model. To navigate this never-ending journey of change, the organization needs to know and update its set of underlying assumptions for how to succeed in the market and industry, then search for or develop new practices fulfilling this new set of assumptions on how to run the business in a digital economy. Because of high uncertainty (you don't know what you don't know), a transformation process requires constant experimentations and refinements of underlying assumptions, espoused values, and implemented practices (artifacts). This cannot be achieved without an active, open-minded search process for new mindsets and practices, as well as transparent communication, involvement, and trust in one another within the company.

References

Schein, E. H. (2010). Organizational culture and leadership (Vol. 2). John Wiley & Sons.

Steiber, A., Alänge, S., Ghosh, S., & Goncalves, D. (2020). *Digital transformation of industrial firms: An innovation diffusion perspective.* European Journal of Innovation Management. https://www.researchgate.net/publication/342212935_Digital_transformation_of_industrial_firms_an_innovation_diffusion_perspective

Venkatraman, N. (1994). *IT-enabled business transformation: From automation to business scope redefinition.* Sloan Management Review, 35(2), 73–87.

About the Author

Dr. Annika Steiber has an MSc in Industrial Economics and Engineering and a PhD in Management of Technology from Chalmers University in Sweden, from where she graduated in the top 1% of the students in her class in 1992. Dr. Steiber has worked as an executive in high-growth companies for almost 20 years and, in parallel, has conducted leading-edge research in the field of management of technology and innovations. Her expertise is in the fields of management for the digital age, innovation management, and transformation of businesses. Dr. Steiber is currently a professor, keynote speaker, advisor, and author of 10 management books and several award-winning research papers. Her latest book, *Leadership for a Digital World: The Transformation of GE Appliances*, was published in 2022 in English and Chinese, as well as an audiobook.

Rethinking Business for the Digital Age

SHEKHAR TANKHIWALE AND HABEEB MAHBOOB

Enterprises have been attempting digital transformations for more than a decade. Despite this, many organizations have yet to complete their digital transformations and are at various stages of digital maturity. A survey conducted by MIT Sloan (Hamberg, 2022) asked respondents (C-level executives) to score their company vis-à-vis the ideal on a scale ranging from 1 to 10. Responses fell into three groups: companies in the early stages of digital development (rating of 1–3 on a 10-point scale, approximately 34% of respondents "mainly talk"); digitally developing companies (rating of 4–6, 41% of respondents, "disjointed actions"); and businesses that are digitally maturing (rating of 7–10, 25% of respondents, "digitally maturing"). The survey reveals that only 25% of the participating company Chief X Officers (the collective name given to the class of corporate executives) believe they are on the path to achieving a higher level of digital maturity. Seventy-five percent of organizations still have much work to be done. The issue gets more complicated because of the lack of a universal definition of what digital transformation entails; additionally, responses from individuals would have been impacted by the lack of a universal scale.

Current Challenges with Digital Transformation

Companies have not been able to achieve higher levels of digital maturity for various reasons: lack of organization-wide digital strategy, leadership buy-in, weak business case, and lack of technology. Various specific issues have also acted as blockers to transforming specific aspects of the organization.

Dependency on obsolete manual processes slows down business flow and makes it difficult for organizations to achieve a higher degree of automation. Mechanization endeavors have not been very successful due to procedural redundancies and integrational pitfalls.

Introducing a platform and module strategy requires a different way of working that reappoints responsibilities within the organization. The journey from a pure project orientation to platform and module responsibilities requires defining several new roles and modifying existing ones.

An outdated catalog, poor end-to-end visibility, waste and unauthorized software, disjointed systems and poor user experience, inability to manage entitlements, and excessive risk and license infringement have hindered the digital transformation of supply chains.

Challenges pertaining to sales and marketing transformation include learning about your customers, generating qualified leads, establishing an omnichannel marketing strategy, and not having a team in place to create content that educates and entertains.

To summarize, various issues—some organization-wide and others specific to a function or process—block organizations from obtaining the full benefits of a digital transformation.

Overcoming Digital Transformation Challenges

Given that a large part of our current work focuses on enabling digital transformation, we have been tracking research and analyzing our experiences on what leads to a successful digital transformation. According to research (Columbus, 2020), enterprise digital maturity is aided by these seven levers: (1) data mastery, (2) intelligent workflows, (3) open talent networks, (4) infrastructure, (5) business model adaptability, (6) unified customer experience, and (7) ecosystem engagement. The levers deliver multipronged business value as measured by revenue, margin, customer satisfaction, product/service quality, and employee engagement. Figure 1 presents the relative impact of individual levers in driving business outcomes.

Of the seven levers, two (data and intelligent workflows) in particular have the biggest impact on driving digital maturity–related business outcomes. Figure 1 shows how ~50% of revenue growth is enabled by these two levers (data and intelligent workflows) alone and 48% by improved customer satisfaction.

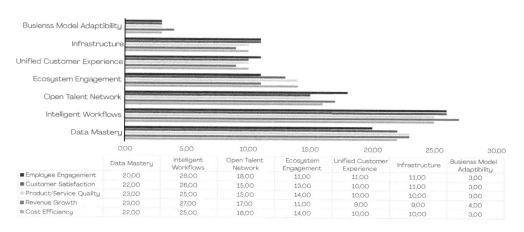

	Data Mastery	Intelligent Workflows	Open Talent Network	Ecosystem Engagement	Unified Customer Experience	Infrastructure	Busienss Model Adaptibility
■ Employee Engagement	20,00	26,00	18,00	11,00	11,00	11,00	3,00
■ Customer Satisfaction	22,00	26,00	15,00	13,00	10,00	11,00	3,00
▦ Product/Service Quality	23,00	25,00	15,00	14,00	10,00	10,00	3,00
■ Revenue Growth	23,00	27,00	17,00	11,00	9,00	9,00	4,00
▦ Cost Efficiency	22,00	25,00	16,00	14,00	10,00	10,00	3,00

Figure 1. Relative impact of individual levers in driving business outcomes.

Our work with clients also confirmed similar themes and made us realize that a unified and integrated approach addressing few critical issues can enable enterprises to obtain the full benefits of digital transformation. This approach also dramatically reduces the time needed to gain value from digital initiatives. We also realized that a clear characterization of the end state is a necessary step to charting the journey. This article discusses our learnings and points of view on the nature of a truly digital enterprise and the pathway to getting there.

Conscious Enterprise: A Business for the Digital Age

Conscious enterprise is our guiding definition of the aspirational end state for a digitally transformed enterprise. Conscious enterprise is the idea that future enterprises, by design, should be able to demonstrate a higher order of sensemaking and action aligned to its purpose than a traditional enterprise

Capabilities That Distinguish a Digitally Transformed Enterprise (Conscious Enterprise)

We identify the few key capabilities that truly distinguish a digital business, which we consider to be the building blocks of a digital business. Figure 2 depicts the capabilities aligned to business goals from an enterprise digital transformation, in other words, zero-touch sales processing, self-healing supply chain, product-as-a-service (PaaS), and virtual twins. All these capabilities align to deliver critical business outcomes that enterprises are looking for.

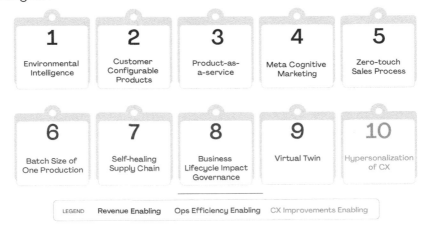

Figure 2. Capabilities for a digitally transformed enterprise (conscious enterprise)

Environmental intelligence pertains to an organization's ability to sense what customers want. Organizations have always struggled to keep track of changing customer preferences. However, with the advent of social media, social listening techniques, and other large-scale data sets, a wide array of information is available for the organization to better understand what their customers want. True digital organizations will have mastered the art of combining external and internal data on almost a real-time basis to adjust organizational direction.

Metacognitive marketing enables organizations to discover the correlation between potential customer desires and the need to nurture them and involves some level of cognitive science. Metacognitive marketing collects data from all possible sources and helps companies identify their potential customers. This eliminates the need for companies to run a broad campaign covering all the customers and helps narrow the campaign focus on the potential buyers. This not only saves costs for the organization but also aids in improving brand image and the campaign's return on investment (ROI). Enterprises that master this capability are precise in crafting marketing messages and targeting offers.

Customer-Configurable Products

Customer-configurable products allow buyers to interactively choose options with a variety of features based on their preferences while ordering. When tied to zero-touch ordering, the process allows customers to design a product to their specific needs. This is a huge help in creating customer advocates.

Nike, Inc., an American multinational corporation offers, among other products, custom-made shoes to its customers. Shoe color, style, and a variety of features can be customized as per the customer's preferences. Besides modular products, inventory automation and real-time inventory tracking enable a rule engine-driven ordering mechanism capability and operationalize customer configurable products. This results in enhanced digital maturity of an organization.

Zero-Touch Sales Processing

Irrespective of their business model (business-to-business or business-to-consumer), organizations are leveraging hyperautomation to enable fully automated sales processing. Even in the B2B space, where a salesperson was traditionally required to navigate the complex decision-making process for the client, companies have shown the power of enabling clients to drive the sales process. Zero-touch ordering is orchestrating automated workflows with a management platform to replace all manual touchpoints. Providing zero-touch automation starts with customer self-service, which provides flexibility to the customer to navigate through the information provided, experience the product on a trial basis and, finally, complete the sales process once decided. This improves customer experience to a great extent. Zero-touch automation relies heavily on big data analytics and predictive analytics to draw insights and take proactive remedial actions, preserving customer experience, operational agility, and cost.

Product-as-a-Service (PaaS), also referred to as product-service systems, is the idea that products are offered in a subscription model or as a service. The product is packaged with more features or service contracts to add newer features, monitor, repair, and even replace. With PaaS, products come in subscription models with services attached. Customers pay a subscription price for the product and pay the recurring fees. PaaS models have more ongoing engagement with closer customer support. Because ownership is not transferred, there is a significant circular economic potential since the company is now responsible for producing a better product. The capabilities required by an organization to master the PaaS model are improved instrumentation on the product, ability for the automatic measurement and wireless transmission of data from remote sources (telemetry), and ability to convert static products into dynamic services to cater to prevailing subscription-based models.

Batch Size of One Production

Enterprises need to significantly rethink their production and logistics operations to serve clients requiring customized/configured products. These include rethinking the product as modular blocks and reimagining the role of the physical point-of-customer interaction (e.g., the dealer). In the discrete manufacturing world, use of cell-based manufacturing enables small lot sizes. This idea needs to be extended across the value chain and lot sizes brought down to their smallest. Enterprises embarking on this journey will also have to rethink how they plan, interact with the supply chain, commit delivery dates to the clients, and so forth. Many luxury car manufacturers (e.g., Bugatti) are good examples of the art of the possible in this direction.

Self-healing supply chains are systems capable of dynamically calculating supply chain performance and optimizing the same. Machine learning (ML) is heavily leveraged in supply chains for a variety of use cases to reduce overall supply chain cost, reduce risk, improve on-time delivery by the suppliers, help reduce the forecast risks, and improve the supply chain planning process. ML algorithms detect high-impact deviations and then show the potential impact on critical business metrics. Self-healing supply chain systems automatically fix incorrect assumptions with predefined thresholds. Finally, self-healing supply chain systems continuously monitor and adjust design parameters over some time, thus closing the gap between expected and actual performance.

Business Life Cycle Impact Governance

Digitally mature organizations build capabilities to get a data-driven holistic view of the business and govern the business while considering all the factors. Although traditional financial metrics and ratios will remain important, conscious enterprises start to measure, report, and manage metrics relevant to society (e.g., environment, healthcare, and safety), employees, and customers. Using data and analytics, these companies are effectively able to combine retrospective (past performance) and forward-looking (prediction) data on performance to plan actions within the company.

Hyperautomated Back Office

Conscious enterprises will take purposeful action and succeed in ensuring straightforward processing of most administrative transactions within the organization. These organizations view any process requiring manual handling as inherently non-scalable. By treating them as technical debt and using multiple automation approaches, digitally mature organizations create back offices that require no human intervention. Most of the services will hence be available as self-service to internal and external stakeholders

Virtual Twin

Digital twin is a virtual representation of the physical assets of a company. Virtual twin will represent the entire company and enable the company to simulate and predict the impacts of various events on the company. These will become real-time tools for managing the company. The many functional implementations we see today (e.g., digital twin, supply chain control tower, digital thread) will merge to form a virtual model of the company. Stakeholders in the company will be able to use the model to predict future performance. These models will be used to conduct impact analyses of various changes. When unplanned events occur, these twins will enable stakeholders to model and quickly plan actions.

In the section above, we have summarized 10 characteristics that will distinguish a business in the digital age. Firms planning digital transformation should use these goals to guide their transformation, which will enable them to develop integrated and holistic roadmaps beyond point-use cases and specific technology-focused conversations.

How to Achieve a Digitally Transformed Enterprise

Becoming a conscious enterprise is a multifaceted complex transformation, spanning multiple business domains (e.g., products, processes, technology, operating model, etc.) that organizations need to undertake to attain all-around improvements in business performance. Achieving the 10 characteristics we detailed in the previous section requires firms to rethink the meta-enablers for the transformation and develop the capabilities to achieve a higher digital maturity level for the organization.

Strategy and Culture

Conscious enterprises view strategy very differently than traditional enterprises. They realize that if they think hard enough and execute well enough around large customer problems, they can build a global-scale enterprise in a very short time. Traditional enterprises need to rethink their strategy-making process and resultant strategy as they become more digital. Traditional constraints to growth (e.g., capital, physical assets such as factories, and hiring of people) are not blockers of a digital enterprise. Digital enterprises realize that if they can identify an approach to unlock significant value for a customer, they will be better equipped to convince customers to switch over and then use the power of network effect to scale the business. In today's world, capital and other resources are readily available for the right opportunity.

Digital companies also build a culture of experimentation, agility, and fail-fast attitude to support this strategy. Digital companies use objectives and key results (OKR) mechanisms to align the company, team, and people goals so that everybody moves in the same direction (e.g., OKR for reducing lead time by one-half is the type of guideline that helps optimize inventory levels).

The Organization as a Network of Pods

Digitally mature organizations rethink their operating models to support the new ways of working. Digitally mature organizations constitute small, self-directed teams working with clearly articulated goals, standards, and game plans to achieve objectives. In these organizations, no single authority or centralized control exists; the control and authority are collectively managed by the members. Successful alignment of business and operating models enables the expeditious implementation of the strategy.

Technology Modularization

The modular IT system platform concept is an extrapolation of systems thinking. The systems thinking framework advocates seeing interrelationships rather than things, models rather than static snapshots. The concept of a platform is also closely related to the modular approach. Modularization allows both portability and interoperability. A module developed once can be repeated in other applications within the platform and operate with other similar or different modules within each application. In addition to being programming neutral, the module is portable and interoperable; it is also programming-language neutral because it incorporates third-party applications to enhance each solution; it also supports the generation of new features, functions, and applications.

Digital enterprises combine technology architectures and platforms that are modular but work together seamlessly. This enables digital enterprises to effortlessly leverage core capabilities while adding new capabilities required to address emerging customer needs.

The Collaborative Anthropomorphic Workforce

Digital enterprises will master the capability to use humans and hard/ soft robots. Anthropomorphism attributes human traits, emotions, or intentions to nonhuman entities. In their quest to hyperautomate, companies increasingly see the possibilities of replacing humans completely, thereby becoming conscious enterprises. Robots, however, will never completely replace human workers and will always serve as an aid to human workers in doing a job that is repetitive and laborious. Intelligent machines will at best acquire human traits, emotions, and intentions but will never completely replace humans; instead, we foresee intelligent machines working collaboratively with humans.

Conscious enterprises rethink their strategy, redesign their operating model, become comfortable operating an andromorphic workforce, and redesign their technology architecture to achieve the 10 characteristics of a digitally mature enterprise.

Where to Start? Digital Maturity Assessment

Digital maturity helps enterprise assess where they stand vis-à-vis digital maturity and what the opportunities are for further digitalization and business value creation. Based on the opportunities identified through a digital maturity assessment, organizations can draw their improvement and value realization roadmap and achieve better outcomes (Rogers, 2016). Figure 3 shows the typical digital maturity assessment output and the scoring on six dimensions and benchmarking of one subdimension (culture).

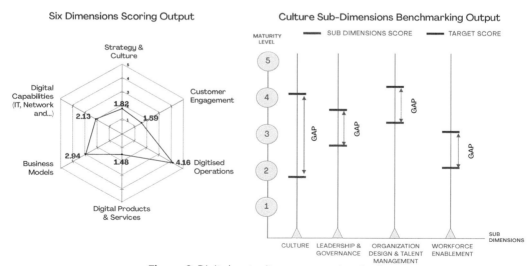

Figure 3. Digital maturity assessment output.

Acknowledgments

The authors would like to acknowledge Nishant Perathara and Sujoy Sen for some stimulating thoughts and ideas for this article.

References

Columbus, L. (2020). *Why digital transformation always needs to start with customers first*. Forbes online. https://www.forbes.com/sites/louiscolumbus/2020/08/30/why-digital-transformation-always-needs-to-start-with-customers-first/?sh=50ae67932c61

Hamberg, L. (2022). *What is digital transformation and digital maturity? Academy of Management Proceedings, Vol. 2022* (1). https://journals.aom.org/doi/abs/10.5465/AMBPP.2022.18172abstract

Rogers, D. (2016). *The digital transformation playbook (5th ed.)*. Columbia University Press.

About the Authors

Dr. Shekhar Tankhiwale works as a Global Managing consultant and Vice President in Tech Mahindra's consulting division, Business Excellence (BE). His focus areas of work are strategy, digital transformation, leveraging of digital technology for business transformation, and business model innovation. He has over 24 years of experience working in the product R&D, manufacturing, and information technology domains; he earned his doctorate (PhD), followed by an MBA with distinction. Shekhar has been an invited speaker for a number of conferences, the recent being the Confederation of Indian Industries (CII) conference on the topic of digital transformation. Shekhar's work has been published in seven international journals on a range of topics, including business model innovation and digital technologies.

Habeeb Mahaboob is a Global Managing Consultant and Senior Vice President with Business Excellence, the consulting and management services practice of Tech Mahindra. Clients typically leverage Habeeb's expertise to identify the impact of (digital) technologies on their businesses (the what) and works with them to devise strategies, operating models, and ways of working (the hows) to address these emerging needs. Habeeb has worked closely with multiple clients to effectively lead the digital agendas of their respective firms. In 2021, *Consulting Magazine* recognized him as one of the global leaders in consulting.

Business Excellence, Inc. is the consulting division of Tech Mahindra. It helps clients achieve their business objectives in the digital age. Tech Mahindra is one of the fastest growing brands among the top 15 IT service providers globally and represents the connected world, offering innovative, customer-centric information technology experiences.

AI-Powered ESG: Our Chance to Make a Real Difference?

TERENCE TSE, MARK ESPOSITO, AND
DANNY GOH

I t is perhaps understandable as to why some people are skeptical about artificial intelligence (AI). First, media and research reports often illustrate how machines will be taking over our jobs, resulting in the elimination of the work positions currently held by many. Second, in many instances, AI remains a "black box." Typically, in machine learning (ML) we can only see the inputs and outputs but are clueless about how those inputs are combined to achieve results. Stated differently, machines turn the input into output in ways that are completely unobservable to us. Applying black box algorithms in various aspects of public lives, such as justice, will have deep social and ethical ramifications. The development of ML technologies is charging full-steam ahead; yet, the methods for monitoring and troubleshooting them are lagging behind.

Third, it appears that some companies, especially the technology giants, have doubled down on AI to increase their profitability, often at the expense of public interest. For example, Google is arguably extracting a staggering amount of data on users' private lives. The company then uses such data to attain accurate predictions of future human behavior, which can subsequently be sold to markets of business customers (Zuboff, 2019). Another (better known) example is how Facebook (now Meta) deployed AI through Cambridge Analytica to influence voters, hence interfering with the democratic processes.

Technology for Good

Yet, we should not forget that AI can also create common benefits. There is no shortage of conversations on how companies can use technologies not just to do good but also to do well. For example, there is an increasing number of discussions on using AI to help reach circular economy goals (McKinsey & Company, 2019; Enel, 2020). Yet, the progress for technology-driven pursuit of sustainability remains slow (Tse, 2020). One reason for such sluggishness is that there remains a lack of economic incentive for companies—and their investors—to make huge investments concerning social and environmental gains and benefits. This also provides an explanation as to why, despite years of discussions on the importance of the so-called triple bottom line—the need to care for not just profit but also people and the planet—has hardly become a mainstream practice among today's businesses. Indeed, at the same time, there is an increasing number of socially and environmentally conscious investors.

Looking at it from this vantage point, two lessons are clear. The first lesson is that, unless investors are getting the satisfactory return, it will be difficult to get businesses to orientate themselves toward goals related to people and the planet. The second lesson is that investors need to have timely and accurate information to make informed decisions. With an increasing number of investors willing to put their capital into projects related to the latest idea in sustainability—environmental, social, and governance (ESG)—the latter problem must be mitigated if not solved. In this respect, AI presents a welcome and potentially extremely beneficial tool to help achieve ESG.

Challenges to Investing in the Socially Important Asset Class

Investments in ESG have fast become an important area of interest. One study points out that sustainable investments amounted to some US$30 trillion in 2018, up by 34% from 2016 (Global Sustainable Alliance, 2019). Indeed, investors (and our societies in general) are increasingly keen to understand whether and by what means businesses are being ESG-compliant. Simultaneously, boards and managements have become cognizant that ESG is crucial to the long-term survival of their companies. It is therefore not surprising that as much as 90% of investors globally are estimated to already have in place, or have plans to develop, specific ESG investment policies (BNY Mellon and the Official Monetary and Financial Institutions Forum [OMFIF], 2020). To guide the selection of such investments, several ESG-based rating and index services, such as MSCI, Bloomberg, and Sustainalytics, have proliferated in recent years.

Unfortunately, investing in ESG is often easier said than done. Investors face at least two challenges: the failures in rating companies and financed emissions, discussed as follows.

Rating companies' failures: Consider the example of the UK-based company, Boohoo. In June 2020, this pioneer of the ultra-fast-fashion retail phenomenon announced a £150 million planned executive bonus. In 2019, the retailer waxed eloquent in its 2019 company report about its "zero-tolerance approach to modern slavery." Yet, shortly thereafter, the company was discovered to be sourcing from a factory in Leicester in which workers were being paid as little as £3.50 per hour (compared to the National Living Wage of £8.72). Equally as bad was the fact that workers had not been provided with proper protective equipment against COVID-19 (Wheeler et al., 2020). Surprisingly, despite these malpractices, Boohoo had received a double A ESG rating from MSCI—its second-highest ranking—while being awarded a far-above industry average score on supply-chain labor standards in its ESG ranking (Mooney & Nilsson, 2020). MSCI is not alone in ranking the fashion retailer highly, however. A review of nine other different ratings placed Boohoo in the top 25th percentile of more than 19,000 companies considered worldwide (Haill, 2020).

Another example is Wirecard, the disgraced German payment processor and financial services provider. While the company filed for bankruptcy in June 2020, news of its questionable business practices broke out as early as 2015. Indeed, until its ultimate collapse, there had been a series of (journalistic) investigations into the company, unearthing ever more evidence of wrongdoings. Yet, throughout all this time, Wirecard received median-grade ratings from a number of ESG ratings agencies (Nauman et al., 2020).

How could the rating companies have gotten it so wrong? The answer: information asymmetry. It appears that all parties in the ratings face different challenges when obtaining and assuring the quality of information. To begin with, rating producers and indices deploy their own proprietary methodologies and data to analyze companies. The results of them using different ESG definitions, measurements, and weightings for different indicators often lead to conclusions and verdicts that can be distinctly different from one index to another. A recent study found that in a dataset of five ESG rating agencies, correlations among scores on 823 companies were on average only 0.61 (Berg et al., 2022). This effectively suggests that, while different rating producers evaluated the same company, their verdicts were usually so differentiated it was as if they were all rating different companies. Indeed, these rating companies mostly rely heavily on information provided by the companies being rated, essentially allowing the latter to feed only favorable data, potentially creating huge biases.

Investors often do not have the resources to conduct in-depth ESG assessments for each of the potential investees. They certainly do not have the time to go through, compare, and reconcile the differences of views and ratings from different suppliers. Without standardization across ratings, it is difficult for investors to compare across the indices created by different providers. Moreover, the fact that interpretation of data by rating companies can be vastly different, often leaving investors to struggle to determine which rating or score would meet their own investment criteria or goals. Another key problem the investors face is that they rely on the rating and index producers to capture the latest information and news and incorporate them into their ratings.

It must be noted that problems are not only restricted to the investors or rating agencies. Investees looking for capital also suffer. For example, because rating criteria and dimensions are determined by the index producers, the companies that are keen to be viewed as ESG-compliant are frequently left wondering how to improve their own ratings. There is also uncertainty over whether investors have enough information to recognize other positive—and negative—factors related to their competitors, which are unaccounted for in the ratings.

Overall, these problems emerge from a lack of clarity, consistency, and transparency of ESG ratings as well as information asymmetry and shortage.

Financed emissions: Financed emissions are emissions generated as a result of financial services, investments, and lending by investors and companies that provide financial services. They fall under scope 3 of the Greenhouse Gas Protocol. A recent report found that the 18 largest U.S. banks and asset managers were responsible for financing the equivalent of 1.97 billion tonnes of CO in 2020. If the U.S. financial sector were a country, it would become the fifth largest global emitter in the world (Sierra Club, 2021). Similarly, the UK financial services sector was estimated to have generated 805 million tonnes of CO through financing in 2019 (Makortoff, 2021). Another report points out that financed emissions account for 700 times more than a financial institution's directly generated emissions (CDP, 2020). The problem is not only the magnitude of pollution. A larger issue is that financed emissions are difficult to track and monitor. Firms face enormous challenges to collect and process data on a continuous basis as well as drawing out insights from it and making them digestible to the end users.

Powering ESG with AI

One potential means of mitigating these issues is to consistently collect qualitative information quickly in order to reinforce the quantitative data already in use. Up-to-date qualitative data has the ability to not only help investors be much better informed; it can also be used to set up key inputs that could be used as the basis to form common minimum standards.

As machines are much more capable than humans to gather and handle qualitative information at scale, cheaply and rapidly, the supply of such information will in turn improve the completeness and timeliness of data and hence the overall quality of ESG data available to investors.

Typically, AI-powered ESG tools follow three steps to produce the desired and insightful output: harvest, organize, and analyze.

Harvest: This step involves parsing ESG-related data. The process starts by using AI to search for and extract company data from a range of sources, including news coverage, messages and postings in social media, expert analyses and third-party ratings, and ESG reports. To do so manually would be a time-consuming, labor-intensive, and costly effort. Even if this were doable, the manual approach to search and import data in real-time fashion on an ongoing basis would be impossible. Indeed, as the universe of ESG data continues to expand exponentially, AI represents the only feasible means to collect and parse data.

Organize: After data collection come screening and entering extracted data into the database. Traditionally, this entails humans to first review the information and then manually key in the data, a process that is demanding in both time and effort; to a great extent, today's technologies make it possible for us to skip this process. Machines can convert a huge volume of such unstructured data into structured data that is readily usable, close to error-free, and swiftly.

More importantly, however, is that AI can collect, organize, and process data that follow the ESG frameworks established by the users and investors, which can vary greatly given different investors have very different investment goals, philosophies, and risk-appetite and evaluation criteria. AI allows them to gather the customized data needed to answer the specifications and requirements of the different investment frameworks. In this way, investors put themselves in the position to produce and continuously update their own designed ratings.

Analyze: The final phase is about discovering and gleaning valuable insights from the structured data set. This involves developing various natural language processing (NLP) techniques such as those related to classifications and taxonomies. It also makes use of analyses that capture sentimental, contextual, and semantic factors embedded in the collected data. This is an essential aspect of putting AI to work to power ESG. As an illustration, an article on a company contains words such as "child labor" or "slavery"; these words certainly carry negative connotations. Yet, in many other articles, they could be sentimentally and semantically unfavorable as a whole, even without the use of words with such connotations. The only way to discern the tone of the information provided is to have humans read each article and then rate whether it is overall positive or negative about a company. Although today's AI technologies have not reached the stage that they can replace humans in playing such roles, they have been progressing fast to become better and better in detecting the embedded contextual information.

Analysis of data is set to become even easier, faster, and more comprehensive with a recent breakthrough in using NLP technologies called the "questions answering model." This is an information-retrieval system, which looks for answers to queries posed by humans and automatically communicates results in a natural language. Using this new technology, a user could simply ask machines questions in the day-to-day language we use for queries, such as: "How does the company's targets and climate change strategy compared to those of peers?" or "What is the carbon emissions of this company?" Properly trained AI models would be able to understand the context and come up with all answers to these questions. This, in turn, has started to help many investors enhance their analyses and produce even more insights.

Machines can also curate up-to-date risk dashboards that enable users to compare extracted data output along various ESG metrics among companies as well as keep track of relevant company news. The outputs produced by all these will be expert-benchmarked and user-defined ESG analyses and ratings that come in the forms of automated reports and reporting.

Is This Our Chance to Make a Real Difference?

None of these is fantasy or science fiction—a new and major initiative is underway in Asia (and more so in Europe) to fashion AI into a tool to collect and process qualitative data. The AI-powered solution seeks to help mine the vast amounts of qualitative, unstructured data through automation. Until now, gathering and gleaning insights from social media, daily local news, and freshly available reports have been slow and labor-intensive activities, fraught with inaccurate results.

The benefits can be huge for all the parties in question. Investors can thus better comply with ESG requirements and make more informed decisions by incorporating ESG data into their investment strategies, for example, by implementing negative/positive screening. Alternately, companies seeking capital are now in a better position to identify and control ESG-related issues and risks, such as improving their company operations and supply chain due diligence, to make themselves more ESG compliant. They can also be reassured that their good deeds will be discernible to investors, quickly and accurately. As for the rating and index providers, real-time signals can offer early warnings and timely indicators, enabling them to produce more accurate updates. Furthermore, these providers can expand the scope of analysis using AI-derived information to complement their current quantitative methods.

While the use of AI to drive ESG is still in its nascent stage and results of the ongoing efforts remain to be seen, history is filled with examples of how technologies have helped attain social goals and create a better society. It is very much hoped that by investor empowerment—particularly those who are ESG orientated—it will be possible for ESG to be a well-respected and common business practice instead of just another fad or slogan advocating sustainability. Just as with fire, AI can be a bad master but a very good servant. Using AI in the right way can no doubt help with our endeavor to raise ethical standards.

References

Berg, F, Koelbel, J. F., & Rigobon, R. (2022). *Aggregate confusion: The divergence of ESG ratings.* Review of Finance, https://doi.org/10.1093/rof/rfac033

BNY Mellon and the Official Monetary and Financial Institutions Forum (OMFIF). (2020). *Global public investor 2020: Sustainable investment.* https://www.omfif.org/esg2020/

CDP. (2020). *The time to green finance.* https://cdn.cdp.net/cdp-production/cms/reports/documents/000/005/741/original/CDP-Financial-Services-Disclosure-Report-2020.pdf?1619537981

Enel. (2020). *Circular economy Enel position paper.* https://www.enel.com/content/dam/enel-com/documenti/azienda/circular-economy-enel-position-paper-en.pdf

Global Sustainable Alliance. (2019). *Global sustainable investment review 2018,* http://www.gsi-alliance.org/wp-content/uploads/2019/03/GSIR_Review2018.3.28.pdf

Haill, O. (2020). *Boohoo factory scandal raises tough questions for ESG and fashion investors, analysts say.* Proactive. https://www.proactiveinvestors.co.uk/companies/news/925162/boohoo-factory-scandal-raises-tough-questions-for-esg-and-fashion-investors-analysts-say-925162.html

Makortoff, K. (2021). *British banks finance 805m tonnes of CO2 production a year.* The Guardian. https://www.theguardian.com/environment/2021/may/25/british-banks-finance-805m-tonnes-of-co2-production-a-year

McKinsey & Co. (2019). *Artificial intelligence and the circular economy: AI as a tool to accelerate the transition.* https://www.mckinsey.com/~/media/McKinsey/Business%20Functions/Sustainability/Our%20Insights/Artificial%20intelligence%20and%20the%20circular%20economy%20AI%20as%20a%20tool%20to%20accelerate%20the%20transition/Artificial-intelligence-and-the-circular-economy.pdf

Mooney, A., & Nilsson, P. (2020). *Why did so many ESG funds back Boohoo? Financial Times.* https://www.ft.com/content/ead7daea-0457-4a0d-9175-93452f0878ec

Nauman, B., Temple-West, P., & Talman, K. (2020). *Did ESG investors pass the Wirecard test? Financial Times.* https://www.ft.com/content/3aeb9395-1f4d-4774-8f4b-5331acc28e04

Sierra Club. (2021). *Wall Street's carbon bubble.* https://static1.squarespace.com/static/61ac8233d16d7417cc6589e3/t/61b84bc6383f9b0e20216046/1639467980190/us_financed_emissions_USL_FIN.pdf

Tse, T. (2020). *On using artificial intelligence to achieve circular economy.* Look Around 2020: Économie Circulaire, https://www2.deloitte.com/content/dam/Deloitte/fr/Documents/sustainability-services/deloitte_escp-look-around-economie-circulaire.pdf

Wheeler, C., Bassey, A., & Matety, V. (2020). *Boohoo: fashion giant faces 'slavery' investigation.* The Times, https://www.thetimes.co.uk/article/booh«oo-fashion-giant-faces-slavery-investigation-57s3hxcth

Zuboff, S. (2019). *The age of surveillance capitalism: The fight for a human future at the new frontier of power.* Profile Books.

About the Authors

Terence Tse is Professor of Finance at Hult International Business School and a co-founder and executive director of Nexus FrontierTech, an AI company. He is also an affiliated professor at ESCP Business School and Cotrugli Business School. He has worked with more than thirty corporate clients and intergovernmental organisations in advisory and training capacities. He has written over 110 articles and three books including The AI Republic: Building the Nexus Between Humans and Intelligent Automation (2019). His latest co-authored work, *The Great Remobilization: Strategies and Designs for a Smarter Global Future*, will be published by MIT Press in October 2023.

Dr. Mark Esposito is Professor of Business & Economics at Hult International Business School, where he directs the Futures Impact Lab. He is also Teaching Faculty at Harvard University's Division of Continuing Education and Affiliate Faculty at the Microeconomics of Competitiveness Program at the Harvard Business School. He serves as Senior Advisor to the Strategy& group at PwC. He is cofounder of Nexus FrontierTech, the Circular Economy Alliance, and Excellere. He is coauthor of *The AI Republic*, *Understanding How the Future Unfolds*, and *The Emerging Economies under the Dome of the Fourth Industrial Revolution*. His latest book, *The Great Remobilization: Strategies and Designs for a Smarter Global Future* will be published by MIT Press in 2023.

Danny Goh is the Founder and CEO of Nexus FrontierTech, an awards-winning company that accelerates enterprise workflows by building AI solutions to automate intensive processes and enable effective use of data and sustainable value creation. He is a coauthor of *The AI Republic: Building the Nexus Between Humans and Intelligent Automation*. Danny is an Entrepreneurship Expert at the Said Business School, University of Oxford and an advisor and judge to several technology start-ups and accelerators. He is a visiting lecturer at various universities in Europe, and a speaker at multiple conferences including TEDx and World Economic Forum.

Disrupting the Disruptors: How Human Capital Makes or Breaks Digital Innovation

RICARDO VIANA VARGAS

Netflix CEO Reed Hastings, considered to be one of the greatest disruptors in the technology sector, suddenly found himself among the ranks of the disrupted. In its 2022 Q2 financial earnings report, Netflix confirmed a net loss of 970,000 subscribers, less than the two million it had predicted but still more than the video streaming giant had ever experienced in a six-month period (Deggans, 2022). As I write this article, over the past year Netflix shares have plunged by 62% and, in a bid to recapture subscribers, the company is now preparing to launch a new lower-cost streaming tier that features four minutes of advertisements for every one hour of content (Canal, 2022).

Hastings is not a casual bystander to the fall in stock price. By some estimates, Hastings personally lost more than US$650 million from the Q1 depreciation stock depreciation on his five million shares (Fabino, 2022).

If the market watchers are correct, there could be more dips in the future (Figure 1).

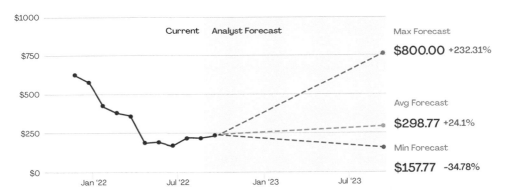

Figure 1. Analyst price target for Netflix stock (NFLX) (Adapted from WallStreetZen. com).

Given his past successes, when Hastings talks, the technology sector listens. So, it was with great interest that in the spring of 2022, Hastings began to do his rounds in the technology media, revealing new plans to create lower-cost subscription tiers that feature advertising, much like some of Netflix's competitors are already doing. "We're going to figure this one out," Hastings said in one interview. "We've got a great team. We lead by a significant margin in streaming, and streaming is continuing to grow around the world" (Brodkin, 2022).

While all of that may be true, the skeptics who were selling their Netflix stock seemed to be preoccupied not with what Hastings was going to do, but why he hadn't done many of those things a long time ago.

As the acknowledged world leader in the subscription video on demand (SVOC) industry, Netflix appeared to be poised to solidify its position when billions of people around the world were forced to shelter at home to escape COVID-19. Social and economic restrictions, and the vast library of original and previously broadcast content available through Netflix, seemed like a match made in heaven.

However, new streaming competitors were arriving on the scene on almost a monthly basis. Suddenly, Netflix found itself in intense competition for subscribers. Add in password sharing—a workaround that Netflix estimated allows 100 million non-subscribers to access its streaming library—and you can see how and where the trouble started brewing.

Today, Netflix continues to lead the streaming pack but its advantage has nearly evaporated (Figure 2).

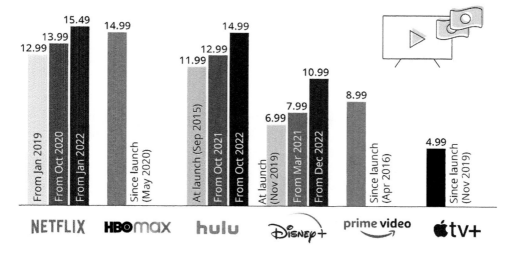

Figure 2. Prices for standard plans including ads-free, high-definition streaming, excluding bundles (Source: Company announcements, Statista).

There are a number of different ways to view the Netflix dilemma. The company continues to represent one of the greatest digital transformation success stories in history, having bet early on video streaming replacing the DVD rental industry. Now, however, the company seems unsure about where its business model is going and how to maintain its dominance.

The circumstantial evidence suggests that Netflix ran into trouble because it stopped looking for new ways to disrupt the marketplace, which allowed competitors to eat away at its business model. More importantly, Netflix did not adequately anticipate how people—primarily its customers but also its employees—would react to increased competition.

It's also unclear whether their current strategy—tempting subscribers with lower monthly fees while also asking them to endure advertisements—will be the ticket to redemption for Hastings. The original value proposition for Netflix was as an ad-free alternative to broadcast television.

It all adds up to an inescapable conclusion: Whether you are just heading out on a digital transformation journey or trying to find ways to maintain your role as a dominant market disruptor, it is the human factor, not the technology that will make or break you. This is a point that somehow continues to evade many business leaders.

The Enduring Failure Rate of Digital Transformations

The high failure rate of digital transformations was a problem long before the pandemic arrived. Most of the major business consultancies—including Boston Consulting Group (BCG), McKinsey & Company, KPMG, and Bain & Company estimated the failure rate for digital transformations at somewhere between 70% and 95%.

Why the failure rate is so high is a point of enduring debate. Some experts point out that digital transformations—projects that require huge financial, technological, and human resources to bring to fruition—take many years to deploy, making them intensely vulnerable to the volatility of market conditions and unanticipated events. Wars, natural disasters and, yes, pandemics, are so seismic in their consequences, they can derail even the most thoughtful transformation strategies.

However, dig deeper and you begin to see that many organizations simply have flawed assumptions about what a digital transformation involves. Many business leaders see it as the deployment of some form of technology. The deeper thinkers in this area debunk that as a dangerous myth that often leads to disaster.

IT researchers Thomas Davenport (Oxford Saïd School of Business) and George Westerman (MIT Sloan School of Management) wrote a seminal analysis of digital transformation failure in 2018. They discovered the businesses that wilted or stumbled in the face of digital transformation had a number of common qualities. They found too many companies wrongly assumed digital transformation would be a cure-all for all the challenges and flaws in their organizations and business plans. In fact, the researchers suggested that, far too often, struggling organizations think their salvation will be found simply by introducing some sort of new technology. Digital capability, the researchers found, is just one of a number of factors (product success, financial market conditions, natural or human-made disruptions) that ultimately determine a company's success or failure. More importantly, Davenport and Westerman noted that many of these failed enterprises were under the impression that digital technologies were plug-and-play solutions. They contend that it is about more than technology (Davenport & Westerman, 2018). On this point, Davenport and Westerman hit on what I think is the biggest missing ingredient in digital transformation: people.

Digital Transformations Fail Because Organizations Still Don't Understand People

To better understand the poor record that many public and private organizations experienced in the commission of major restructurings or transformations, the Project Management Institute created the Brightline® Initiative, a partnership involving some of the world's leading consulting and human capital firms, leaders in pharmaceuticals and communications, along with leading business schools. The idea was to help senior leadership in both the public and private sectors recognize that people form the link between strategy, design, and delivery: they turn ideas into reality; they are the strategy in motion.

To emphasize the importance of human capital, and to acknowledge the failure to take full advantage of this critical resource, Brightline® created its *People Manifesto*. In short, the manifesto is a series of important concepts that amplify the importance of human capital in project management and a blueprint for how organizations can re-imagine their culture and strategy execution. There are four major pillars to the manifesto:

Pillar 1: Leadership is overemphasized. Most of the business world understands that strong leadership is necessary for success. However, it is just as important that senior leadership knows not only when to lead, but also when to follow. This is also a recognition that strong leadership is more of a liability than an asset if the people in your organization are not motivated to follow.

Pillar 2: Collaboration is important, but it's not everything. Promoting a collaborative team culture, while breaking down silos and encouraging a one-company mindset, are some of the most emphasized elements of organizational culture. However, it's important to remember that good teams are an assembly of people with different but complimentary skill sets. The fact is, not all initiatives require a "team effort." Sometimes, individuals should be allowed to do what they do best, and drive a project forward on their own.

Pillar 3: Culture is not built; it must be cultivated. So many organizations and consultants talk about how to "build" a culture of success. In fact, culture is a dynamic and living organism that is the product of the tension between individual behaviors and responses. To fully align culture with strategy, there must be a shared sense of purpose and trust. A safe, productive and innovative culture cannot be left to chance; it must be cultivated by putting the right people in the right environment.

Pillar 4: People act in their own self-interest. So many leadership advisors caution against self-interest, describing it as a dangerous and destructive force. And, while that may be true, you cannot simply ban self-interest; it is an essential and enduring part of the human condition. The best organizations recognize how self-interest sometimes derails project management and craft responses that are specifically designed to shift individual interests, mindsets, and behaviors.

How to Harness the Power of People to Drive Digital Transformation

The principal focus of digital transformation will almost always be on the technology; yet, it is the ability of the people of an organization to absorb and exploit that technology, which makes or breaks a transformation. In short, all that leading-edge technology will be squandered unless an organization can harness the power of human nature.

In 2019, author and transformation expert Benham Tabrizi and colleagues from Minicircuits, a global manufacturer of radio frequency and microwave components, identified five key lessons from failed digital transformations. Two of those five involved overlooked considerations around human capital.

> "Why do some DT efforts succeed and others fail?" Tabrizi and his colleagues ask in the introduction to an article in the *Harvard Business Review*. "Fundamentally, it's because most digital technologies provide *possibilities* for efficiency gains and customer intimacy. But if people lack the right mindset to change and the current organizational practices are flawed, DT will simply magnify those flaws" (Tabrizi et al., 2019).

The best organizations all have the following similar approaches to digital transformation that, when applied appropriately, create the greatest chances for success:

1. **Don't leave people in the dark.** When digital transformations are designed they often leave out a communications strategy on the basis that key information on what, how, and when should only be available to some people on a need-to-know basis. The fact is, everyone affected by the transformation needs to know. Make

sure a communications strategy is part of the inception of the transformation. Don't allow your leaders to hoard all the information and leave the majority of people in the dark.

2. **Focus on quick wins rather than a big bang.** Some of the most promising digital transformations have come undone, because leadership decided it could not reveal part of the transformation until the entire initiative was ready to go. However, delivering quick wins— partial implementation or an iterative rollout of a larger project— allows people to see the transformation vision in real time. It takes the conceptual and makes it the concrete. That will build support and enthusiasm. Keeping everything under wraps until everything is completed will only cultivate anxiety and dissent.

3. **Remember, it's not just the what, it's the why.** Are you undertaking a transformation just to keep up with competitors? Or, perhaps the end goal is to completely reinvent what you are doing and how you are doing it. You need to explain to your people why you are taking this journey and—most importantly—what the consequences will be for your workers. Give people time not only to accept what is happening, but plan for the future. Even if that future is not with your organization.

4. **Confront fear head-on.** The first feeling that many people will have when they hear the words "digital transformation" is fear. They will fear the loss of their jobs and livelihoods, perhaps to some form of technology that will be able to do exactly what they are doing, but cheaper and faster. Or, the loss of a job they love. They also fear that they do not have the capacity to learn new skills to future- proof their careers. Organizations must acknowledge this fear and speak to it upfront in any transformation. Fear that is left to fester can only threaten the successful completion of any transformation. Remember, in any digital transformation, technology is the easy part; changing mindsets and behaviors is the real challenge.

5. **Always remember the threats posed by unforeseen events.** With global pandemics, climate change, and geopolitics, we are reminded that life is volatile and unpredictable. So, the business model of the future that you created today may no longer be viable in six months. Organizations must be agile and adaptable. They must build contingencies into their digital transformations that allow for unforeseen events and quick changes in direction. Do not forge ahead with an outdated plan because you're afraid to admit conditions have changed. Adapt and survive.

Even as New Technologies Arrive, the Importance of a Skilled and Motivated Workforce Cannot be Ignored

Trying to find the best way of using technology to build a business plan for the future can seem like a daunting task. Which technology and applied in what fashion? Do I need to provide employees with better digital tools or start replacing some of them with artificial intelligence (AI)—inspired solutions? Fortunately, some the world's most successful technology companies have actually shown us the way: to become a true disruptor, you must involve equal parts technology and human capital.

With every new digital solution or tool, there must be skilled and creative human hands helping people decide how best to use it. Yes, digital technologies and machine learning (ML) are replacing the human touch in some jobs. That is as inevitable as any future business trend. But AI won't replace all jobs, which means you need the right people with the right skills to help you extract the greatest value from any digital investment.

The future is bright for businesses that understand the need for more and better concurrent investment in technology and human capital. For those who do not grasp that equation, there will be a short, sharp journey to business oblivion.

References

Brodkin, J. (2022). *Netflix stock plummets 37% as CEO says company plans ad-supported tier.* Arstechnica.com

Canal A. (2022). *Netflix's new ad-supported tier will return company to growth: Analyst.* Yahoo Finance.

Davenport, T., & Westerman, G. (2018). *Why so many high-profile digital transformations fail.* Harvard Business Review. https://hbr.org/2018/03/why-so-many-high-profile-digital-transformations-fail

Deggans, E. (2022). *Netflix loses nearly 1 million subscribers.* NPR

Fabino, A. J. (2022). *Here's how much Reed Hastings, Bill Ackman and Baillie Gifford lost on the Netflix plunge.* Benzinga.com

Tabrizi, B., Lam, E., Girard, K., & Irwin, V. (2019). *Digital transformation is not about technology.* Harvard Business Review. https://hbr.org/2019/03/digital-transformation-is-not-about-technology

About the Author

Ricardo Viana Vargas, PhD is an experienced leader in global operations, project management, business transformation and crisis management. Founder and managing director of Macrosolutions, a consulting firm with international operations in energy, infrastructure, IT, oil and finance, he managed more than US$20 billion in international projects in the past 25 years. Former chairman of the Project Management Institute (PMI), Ricardo created and led the Brightline® Initiative from 2016 to 2020 and was the director of project management and infrastructure at the United Nations, leading more than 1,000 projects in humanitarian and development projects.

He wrote 16 books in the field, has delivered 250 keynote addresses in 40 countries, and hosts the "5 Minutes Podcast," which has reached 12 million views. Ricardo holds a PhD in Civil Engineering, a master's in Industrial Engineering, and an undergraduate degree in Chemical Engineering.